Walking by Faith

by Roy E. Cogdill

ONE STONE
BIBLICAL RESOURCES

Published by:
One Stone Press
979 Lovers Lane
Bowling Green, KY 42103

Printed in the United States of America

ISBN: 978-1-941422-66-3

ONE STONE
BIBLICAL RESOURCES

www.onestone.com

Foreword

For nearly two decades *The New Testament Church* has been used by congregations of Christians all over the world as a sound and highly valuable textbook for adult classes. Its outline lessons on the church have never been questioned as to their scripturalness and their fidelity to the New Testament in every particular.

The same author now gives us *Walking by Faith*, which is a sequel to his former work, and is in particular an amplification and application of certain lessons contained in outline in *The New Testament Church*. Whereas the earlier book simply gave the outline, without making application to particular practices and situations, this latter one applies the principles and truths to situations and conditions.

Roy E. Cogdill is eminently fitted for the task of producing such a work as this. For nearly thirty-five years he has been a preacher of the gospel and almost from the start has been regarded as one of the ablest teachers in the church. He has held gospel meetings in every part of the nation, as well as having spent prolonged periods in evangelism in Canada. He knows the problems that churches face; he knows the teaching of God's word which deals with those problems, and he knows how to apply the one to the other. Such he has done in *Walking by Faith*.

When controversy and differences are on every hand and when the peace of God's people is jeopardized, it is highly proper that such a class book as *Walking by Faith* be placed in the hands of every child of God. Churches may wisely conduct earnest and careful studies of controverted points, sifting truth from error, striving constantly to bring forth the exact teaching of God's word on all matters of difference. The two fundamental concepts which Christians have always held—the absolute authority of the word and the firm conviction that the word can be understood—make it forever impossible that God's people shall divide over any point of Bible teaching. For when any difference arises among them, they immediately resort to the Bible with the query, "What saith the Scriptures?" And they continue their study until there is unity of understanding as to Bible teaching. Once that unity is reached, the matter is settled.

Walking by Faith will prove invaluable in such a study. It is prepared for the very purpose of eliciting Bible truth on certain controverted questions. The open mind and the honest heart cannot fail to be helped by its use.

— *Fanning Yater Tant (1957)*

Author's Note

In this work no claim is made for perfection. There are likely some mistakes that will need correction and in later editions such mistakes as are discovered will be corrected.

The desire has been only to furnish to the student of God's word a guide in the study of the Scriptures concerning the issues that are involved in the nature, organization, and work of the church and in scriptural cooperation among the churches of Christ.

Every major apostasy in the history of the church has begun in a corruption of the government of God's people. Respect for divine authority must first be destroyed in the hearts of God's people or they will not depart from his ways. This being true, every Christian must be a careful and prayerful student of what God's word teaches on these matters.

Those who reverence the will of God and respect his word as Christians must will not be stampeded by the wisdom of men, traditions, or customs, however ancient they may be, or by sentiment, emotion or popularity. They will rather "search the scriptures" and "give diligence to shew (themselves) approved unto God (workmen) that needeth not to be ashamed, rightly dividing the word of Truth." May God help us in this and every other study to "prove all things; hold fast that which is good."

"Buy the truth and sell it not."

— *Roy E. Cogdill*

Table of Contents

The Mission of the Church

INTRODUCTION

This lesson emphasizes the church as a divine arrangement with a divine arrangement with a divine purpose. This fact should dispel from every mind the common concept that the church was planned by human wisdom, brought into existence by human will or ruled by human authority.

I.   **The church is the result of God's eternal purpose.**

1.   The manifestation of God's wisdom which had remained a mystery from eternity is now made known in the preaching of the gospel of Christ and in the very existence of the church as a part of God's plan (Ephesians 3:8-10).

2.   Such was the purpose and plan of God from eternity (Ephesians 3:11).

3.   God, then, is the supreme architect of the church.

     (1)   The pattern is divine—the result of divine wisdom and planning. Just as the strength and beauty of a great building manifests the wisdom of the architect, and a great feat of engineering, such as a great bridge, evidences the wisdom of the engineer, so the church evidences in its very nature and existence the wisdom of the God of heaven who planned it.

     (2)   The pattern represents not only divine planning but divine will which cannot be disregarded but must be followed. Note these examples:

           a.   God gave Noah a pattern for the ark (Genesis 6:13-22). Noah followed the pattern and was saved (Genesis 7:1-5; 1 Peter 3:20; Hebrews 11:7).

           b.   Moses was instructed to build the tabernacle according to the pattern God gave him (Exodus 25:9-40; Exodus 26:30; Numbers 8:4).

           c.   God gave the pattern for bearing the ark of the covenant (Exodus 25:14; Exodus 37:5). David did not follow the divine pattern and Uzzah lost his life when he touched the ark (2 Samuel 6:3). David acknowledged his mistake and sought to rectify it (1 Chronicles 15:11-15).

   d. Israel departed from the pattern God gave and was condemned as a result (Acts 7:37-44).

   e. This principle is applied to the church (Hebrews 8:1-5; 1 Corinthians 3:9-17).

   f. The idea that God tells us only what to do and not how to do it is in direct conflict with Bible teaching.

4. The church is the "tabernacle which the Lord has pitched and not man," built by Christ in harmony with God's purpose and plan.

Matthew 16:18—"I will build my church."

Hebrews 8:1-5—Build it according to the pattern.

5. Ruled by divine will and authority.

   (1) All authority belongs to Christ in this age (Matthew 28:18-20).

   (2) He is the head over "all things to the church"—no other authority in the church but his (Ephesians 1:18-23).

   (3) Whatever the church is and does, Christ must have willed it.

II. There is a divine plan for the church in accomplishing God's purposes (Ephesians 4:11).

1. **Apostles** and **prophets**—Theirs was the work of divine revelation, making known the will of God. We have their work preserved in the providence of God in the New Testament and it is accessible in its completeness.

2. **Evangelists**—Theirs was the work of propagating the gospel.

3. **Pastors** and **teachers**—Their work was within the congregation. The pastors, bishops, and elders were all the same. This same word in the Greek—pastors here, *poimenas*—occurs in Acts 20:28 and is translated "feed" or shepherd.

4. Divine wisdom has given this arrangement through which the church is to accomplish its divine mission.

5. Those who were charged with the performance of these tasks in the early church were given "gifts" to make it possible for them to function according to the divine will until revelation was completed.

Ephesians 4:8   "When he ascended up on high he gave gifts unto men."

Ephesians 4:11   "He gave some apostles," etc.

Ephesians 4:13   "till we all come in unity of the faith, and of the knowledge of the Son of God, unto a perfect man, unto the measure of the stature of the fulness of Christ" (this denotes the completeness of revelation).

III. The church has been given a divine program of work or activity (Ephesians 4:12).

1. **"For the perfecting of the saints."** The word "perfecting" is from the Greek *katartismon* which MacKnight says "properly signified to place the parts of any machine or body in their proper order and to unite them in such a manner as to render the machine or body complete." This indicates then what we call the work of edifying the body—the work of educating or training Christians in right living and acceptable service to God. A later lesson will deal particularly with this mission of the church.

2. **"For the work of the ministry."** Here "ministry" comes from the Greek *diakonia.* It occurs in 2 Corinthians 9:1; 11:8, and many other passages and is translated both as "ministers" and "serve." It is the word translated "deacon." Service is the idea. It includes ministering to the poor but is in no wise limited to that. It includes any service rendered in behalf of anyone needing help whether in a physical or spiritual matter. Here is the field of good works in the Christian's own individual life. A later lesson will be directed to this phase of the mission of the church.

3. **"Unto the building up of the body of Christ"** (ASV). This is the same word used by Jesus in Matthew 16:18—*oikodomeo*—(in verb form) when he promised to "build my church." Evidently Paul uses it here in the sense of plant, establish where it is not known, enlarge the borders thereof by bringing others into it by the preaching of the gospel. It sets forth that a primary work of the church is evangelizing the world with the gospel.

IV. What the mission of the church is not.

1. **The mission of the church is not social.** Christianity is not a "social religion." The gospel of Christ is not a "social gospel." The church of the Lord is not a "social institution." While the gospel, with its principles of everlasting truth, will work in social reform, it does so by reforming the individual's manner of living and thinking. Christianity did not undertake social reform or social guidance in the New Testament age. The church did not become

a social institution or the center of social activity. It did not wage a campaign for social reformation or social equality.

(1) Paul taught that, if Christianity found a man either slave or master, it was to make a better one out of him (1 Corinthians 7:20-22).

(2) He also taught that the home is to be the center of social activity, not the church (1 Corinthians 11:20-22).

(3) The increasing tendency to socialize church services and church work by having "fellowship banquets," a social hour with refreshments after the service for various groups, a church dining room, parlor, or cafeteria to entertain visitors and accommodate social functions, serving refreshments between Bible classes and worship to attract greater attendance is purely sectarian and leads directly to what Paul condemned upon the part of the Corinthians.

(4) Certainly there is good to be derived from Christians associating and eating together but it should be kept on the basis of home and individual Christian activity and not church activity.

2. **It is not the business or work of the church to provide and serve as guide in recreational activity.** Church basketball teams, church sponsored skating parties and swimming parties, facilities for ping-pong games and the like are a perversion of the energies and resources of the church. It isn't the business of the church to furnish entertainment or recreation for either young or old.

3. **Making money is not the function of the church.** The church has no business in business. God gave the pattern for raising the funds to do the work of the church (1 Corinthians 16:1-2). It should be respected. Merchandising, manufacturing, farming, or any other economic endeavor is outside the function and work of the Lord's church. All legitimate business should be kept in the field of individual enterprise.

4. **The church is not a court or school of domestic relations.** Whatever the Bible teaches should be taught whenever and wherever it is needed by any Christian and by the church. But parent education, psychology, pedagogy, sociology, and such related subjects that are not taught in the word of God are not the task of the church. Preachers who make a specialty of love, courtship, marriage, parent education, and counseling those who

are having difficulty in domestic relations and in social problems should do such work in some other way than through the church and should not deceive themselves into thinking that such work is the work of a gospel preacher.

5. **Secular education—the teaching of secular subjects such as science, mathematics, history, literature, etc.—does not come within the scope of the mission and work of the church and should be made no part of its work.**

6. **Political issues do not belong in the church.** God ordained civil government to meet all such issues and resolve them and they should be left there (Romans 13:1-7; 1 Peter 2:13-17).

CONCLUSION

No man has the right to prostitute the energy, strength, zeal or resources of the church of our Lord to serve human aims or purposes. The church should be kept faithful to the divine mission that was God's purpose from eternity for her to serve.

The Sufficiency of the Church of Christ

INTRODUCTION

If the church of our Lord is **sufficient** to accomplish what the Lord intended for it to do, it is **competent**, **adequate** and no other organization or arrangement is permitted, much less needed. Any effort made by man to add or improve upon the Lord's arrangement for the accomplishment of his purpose through his church indicates dissatisfaction with God's ways.

I. **The church is a divine plan executed (review Lesson 1).**

   1. The church is a tabernacle which the Lord has pitched and not man (Hebrews 8:1-5).

      (1) God is the divine architect and Christ is the builder. There can be no deviation from the divine pattern without condemnation (1 Corinthians 3:9-11).

   2. The fulfillment of God's eternal purpose (Ephesians 3:8-11; Colossians 1:23-28).

   3. Foretold by the prophets (Isaiah 2:2-5; 28:16; 1 Peter 2:5-10).

   4. Prepared for by John the Baptist and during the personal ministry of the Lord (Isaiah 40:3-5; Matthew 3:1-3; 10:5-7).

   5. Christ promised to build it (Matthew 16:13-20).

   6. The church in existence (Acts 2:47; 5:11; 11:26).

II. **The church designed by divine wisdom for a divine purpose must be sufficient to accomplish that purpose.**

   1. To deny the sufficiency of the church is to impeach the wisdom of God in his divine plan and program (1 Corinthians 1:25-31; Romans 11:33-36; 16:27; Acts 15:18).

   2. In order to improve upon this divine arrangement man would have to be wiser than God (Jeremiah 10:23; 1 Corinthians 3:19; Matthew 15:13-14; Galatians 1:6-8; Romans 9:20).

III. The church revealed by the Holy Spirit in God's perfect revelation must be sufficient.

1. Divine revelation makes known all of God's will concerning man's redemption.

    (1) All truth revealed by the Holy Spirit through apostles (John 14:26).

    (2) All things that pertain to life and godliness (2 Peter 1:3).

    (3) God's righteousness completely revealed therein (Romans 1:16-17).

    (4) Altogether profitable for every need (2 Timothy 3:14-17).

    (5) By the testimony of the Holy Spirit only can man know the mind of God (1 Corinthians 2:10-12).

    (6) Perfection—completeness—is found in Christ and his word (Colossians 2:10).

2. Divine revelation sets forth God's ways.

    (1) "Teaching them to observe whatsoever I have commanded you" (Matthew 28:20).

    (2) Paul certified that the gospel preached by him was a revelation of the Lord and condemned man to perdition who perverted it in any way (Galatians 1:6-12).

    (3) The things received of Paul to be committed unto faithful men who would teach them to others (2 Timothy 2:2).

    (4) Not to go beyond the things written (1 Corinthians 4:6; 2 Corinthians 4:13; 1 Thessalonians 1:6; 2 Thessalonians 3:6-14).

3. A perfect revelation cannot set forth imperfect ways nor an imperfect and insufficient institution. God's ways revealed in God's word are sufficient to accomplish God's purposes (Romans 11:33-36).

IV. The function of the church is under divine authority and supervision.

1. Christ is the head over all things to it (Ephesians 1:21-23). As his body, its members are so related that their every function is directed by him. No member of the human body can normally perform its function without the direction of the brain (Romans 12:3-6). Each member is to perform his function by faith or in accordance with the Lord's instructions (2 Corinthians 5:7;

1 Corinthians 12:12-13). God has arranged the body to please him (1 Corinthians 12:24-28).

2. The Holy Spirit dwells in the church as long as the church is subject to his leading (Ephesians 2:18; Romans 8:9-18).

3. The apostolic office constitutes the supreme court in the church and it is bound by their decisions (Matthew 19:29; Acts 15). The apostles settled the question of circumcision (Galatians 2).

V. **The church as God designed it, as Christ built it, and as the Holy Spirit has revealed it represents God's ways and they are always not only sufficient but they are best (Jeremiah 10:23; Proverbs 16:25; Isaiah 55:8-9; Deuteronomy 8:6; 26:17; 28:9; 30:16).**

1. God's ways are best because God's wisdom is infinite and he knows best.

2. God's ways are best because God can always see the end of a way from the beginning.

3. God's ways are best because God is always guided by his love for us and our good in choosing them for us.

4. God's ways are best because they honor God and are an indication of our faith and trust in him.

5. God's ways are best for they always serve his purpose.

CONCLUSION

Any effort to improve upon God's ways represents unbelief. Any deviation means we have turned away from God's ways to man's ways.

How Scriptural Authority Can Be Established

INTRODUCTION

Authority is the right to command or direct and enforce obedience or administer punishment. To authorize a thing is to empower to act, or direct by authority. In divine affairs, all authority inheres in God.

I. **God has given to Christ absolute authority in the church.**

    1. He is God's lawgiver to his people today (Hebrews 1:1-2; Acts 3:22-25).

    2. "All authority" given into his hands (Matthew 28:18). Includes legislative, executive, and judicial.

    3. He is "head over all things to the church which is his body" (Ephesians 1:21-23).

        (1) Can act in the church only by his authority.

            a. Head controls the body.

            b. Church absolute monarchy. Christ is king (Ephesians 1:19-21; Colossians 1:18-19).

            c. Forbidden to go beyond his word (2 John 9, 11).

        (2) Walk in him (Colossians 2:6-10).

II. **Christ gave binding and loosing authority only to his apostles.**

    1. Matthew 15:1-9.

        (1) Human authority makes worship vain (Matthew 15:8-9).

        (2) Human authority shall be rooted up (Matthew 15:13).

        (3) Human teachers are blind guides of the blind (Matthew 15:14).

            a. Jesus respected and kept the law of God but did not keep those things bound by the traditions of the elders—washing hands (Matthew 15:1-9).

            b. Jesus condemned the Jewish elders for presuming to release men from what the law of God bound (Matthew 15:4-6).

    2. Heaven respects only the authority of Christ through the apostles (Matthew 16:19).

       (1) All obligations and all liberty in the church of our Lord is prescribed by apostolic authority. No man has any right to go beyond in either direction.

3. Proper respect for the authority of Christ can be shown only by respecting the authority of apostles (John 13:20; 20:22-23; 1 John 4:6; Matthew 19:29).

4. Differences on the question of circumcision settled by apostles in Jerusalem (Galatians 2:1-3; Acts 15:1-31). This is the method of settling every question that arises in the church today.

III. The authority of Christ exercised by the apostles completely in New Testament Scriptures.

1. The Scriptures are perfect and complete, therefore sufficient (2 Peter 1:3; 2 Timothy 3:13-17; Jude 3).

2. We are forbidden to go beyond (Galatians 1:6-8; 2 John 9-11; 1 Corinthians 14:37).

3. We must follow the apostolic pattern (Philippians 3:16-19; 4:9; 1 Thessalonians 2:14; 1 Corinthians 4:16-17; Matthew 28:20).

IV. How to establish authority from New Testament scriptures.

1. **By precept.** By this we mean direct statement or positive command.

2. **By approved example.** By this we mean the practice of the church in the New Testament under apostolic guidance and which the apostles had received from the Lord and therefore by divine appointment.

3. **Necessary inference.** That which though neither expressly stated nor specifically exemplified yet is necessarily implied by the clear import and meaning of the language used.

       (1) These three methods of receiving divine authority illustrated by the Lord's supper:

          a. **Precept**—its observance. "This do in remembrance of me" (1 Corinthians 11:25).

             (a) Paul received it of the Lord and gave it to the church by his authority (1 Corinthians 11:23). "Teaching them to observe all things whatsoever I have commanded you" (Matthew 28:20).

          b. **Approved example**—the time of its observance. "And upon the first day of the week, when the disciples came together to break bread" (Acts 20:7).

(a) Paul had received this memorial institution from the Lord and knew therefore when the Lord wanted it to be observed.

(b) He remained in Troas for seven days, obviously waiting for the day upon which the saints assembled (Acts 20:6).

(c) This evidences that the Lord's supper was observed in the church of the New Testament days only upon the first day of the week, the Lord's day (Revelation 1:10).

c. **Necessary inference**—the frequency of its observance. "The first day of the week to break bread."

Compare:

"Remember the Sabbath day to keep it holy" (Exodus 20:8).

"The first day of the week to break bread" (Acts 20:7).

Note: If the "Sabbath day to keep it holy" means every Sabbath, as regularly as it comes, then "the first day of the week to break bread" means every "first day," as regularly as it comes. This is the unavoidable implication of the clear import and meaning of the language used. There is no other way of determining how often this memorial supper is to be observed.

V. **Generic and specific authority.** All authority is either **general**—including any thing, method, or means of execution that comes within the class or order of the precept, example or thing commanded; or **specific**—excluding every thing, method, or means of execution in the same order or class which is not particularly specified in the precept, example or thing commanded. General authority *includes*; specific authority *excludes*.

1. This principle illustrated:

(1) **"Go"** (Matthew 28:19).

How?	Which?
Walk • Ride • Fly • Sail	God did not specify. He gave us the choice. No man has the right to bind a specific method.

(2) **"Teach"** (Matthew 28:19-20).

How?	Which?
Private • Public • Class	God did not specify. He gave us the choice. No man has the right to bind a specific method.

(3) **"Assemble"** (Hebrews 10:25).

Where?	Which?
Home • Rented hall Own meeting house	God did not specify. Left to man's judgment to select most expedient.

(4) **"Sing"** (Ephesians 5:19; Colossians 3:16).

How?	Which?
With book • By memory	God did not specify but left the choice to man's judgment. No man has the right to legislate or specify.
What part? Soprano • Alto • Tenor • Bass	

2. Instances of specific authority excluding:

(1) **Noah's ark.** Build it of gopher wood (Genesis 6:14).

Gopher wood excluded:	Which?
Walnut • Pine • Ash • Spruce All other kinds	God specified gopher. No man had the right to add another kind.

(2) **The water of cleansing.** The ashes of a red heifer (Numbers 19:2).

A red heifer excluded:	Which?
Sheep • Goat • Pig • Horse Camel • Every other color of heifer	God specified not only the kind of animal but even the color. No man had the right to add another color or kind.

(3) **Sing** (Ephesians 5:19). Excludes every other "kind" of music. Instrumental music is excluded by the fact that God specified "sing" and that does not include "playing" an instrument. No man has the right to grant a liberty which God's authority excludes.

(4) **The Lord's Supper** (Acts 20:7; 1 Corinthians 11:23). The unleavened loaf and fruit of the vine excluded every other element. The first day of the week excluded every other day. God has made the choice with reference to these matters and man has none but to do the will of God or rebel.

(5) **The congregation** (Acts 14:23; Philippians 1:1). God has specified congregational government under elders or bishops. There is nothing larger or smaller in the New Testament Scriptures. There is nothing else. Man has to accept God's arrangement and be satisfied or rebel against divine authority by substituting or adding some other organization.

(6) **Elders in every church** (Acts 20:28; 1 Peter 5:2). God has specified the jurisdiction of elders. They are to "feed the flock of God which is among you, taking the oversight thereof" (1 Peter 5:2). They are to "take heed to the flock over the which the Holy Spirit hath made you overseers" (Acts 20:28). Whenever elders become overseers of anything else but the work of the flock "which is among them" or the "flock over the which the Holy Spirit made them overseers" they are without jurisdiction as elders and have therefore added to the word of God.

CONCLUSION

In order for a thing to be authorized there must be either **precept**, **approved example**, or **necessary inference** in New Testament Scriptures. If the means of authority is general, then anything included within the scope of the thing authorized is permissible. But if God specified the kind or the method of execution, then no substitute or addition is allowed but everything of the same class or order is excluded. In such cases God has left man no choice but to respect God's stipulations by obeying his word or rebelling against divine authority by substituting or adding of his own will.

There are two extremes in consideration of divine authority. One extreme position is taken by the Anti-Sunday School group of brethren who contend that, in order for a thing to be scriptural, it must be specifically authorized. Upon this basis they reject the class system of teaching. The other extreme is taken by the "digressive" brethren of the Christian Church group who contend that in order for a thing to be wrong it must be specifically condemned. Both are wrong. One binds where God has not bound and the other looses where God has bound.

The Bible Doctrine of Expediency

INTRODUCTION

Men have sought to justify a multitude of things by the claim that they can be practiced as expediencies. The common conception seems to be that the end justifies the means and anything that will accomplish what we seem to think to be good whether it is authorized or not is permissible. In order for a thing to be a scriptural expedient in spiritual affairs it must facilitate in the accomplishment of God's will and must be in harmony with his word.

I. **In order for a thing to be expedient it must be lawful.**

1. **1 Corinthians 6:12; 10:23.** These passages teach that expediency must come within the realm of that which is lawful. If a thing does not come within the scope of that which is authorized—if there is no precept, approved example, or necessary inference in the Scriptures which authorize the practice—then there is no divine authority for it. That which is unauthorized is unlawful— prohibited—by divine authority and is, therefore, sinful. Such involves going beyond the word of the Lord (2 John 9-11) and is consequently beyond the realm of faith (2 Corinthians 5:7; Romans 14:23). The silence of God must be respected. We cannot have any assurance that anything is pleasing to God unless the Holy Spirit has borne such testimony (1 Corinthians 2:10-13). When we have no assurance that a thing is pleasing in God's sight, to practice it is presumption, and God has always condemned presumption as sinful. Consider the Old Testament examples of Cain (Genesis 4), Nadab and Abihu (Leviticus 10:1-2), Uzzah (2 Samuel 6:6-7), and Uzziah (2 Chronicles 26:18-21).

II. **For a thing to be expedient it cannot be specified.**

1. When God specifies, there is no choice but to obey or disobey. In matters specified, faith demands obedience. Expediency in human wisdom involves the right of a choice within the realm of those things included in what God has authorized.

    (1) To go beyond that which is specified or offer a substitute therefore is to **add** to what God has said instead of **aiding** obedience to his word.

a. God commands "sing"—instrumental music is not an **aid** in "singing" but is an **addition** to God's commandment. It is not included in the scope of the commandment and is, therefore, unauthorized and cannot be practiced "by faith."

b. God commands to dip (*baptizo*), bury (Romans 6:4) in baptism. Sprinkling is not an **aid** in carrying out that command. It does not expedite in carrying out God's command but is a **substitute** for what God said do. A baptistry might expedite and, therefore, aid in obeying God's commandment, but it does not add to or substitute therefor.

c. A missionary society or any other organization that men build and maintain to do the work of God's church is not an **aid** in carrying out God's commandment. It is an **addition** or a **substitute** for the Lord's way, because it does not come within the scope of the organization specified in the word of the Lord—the congregation under its own elders (Acts 14:23; Philippians 1:1).

d. For elders of the Lord's church to take jurisdiction over the work of a number of congregations or supervise some human institution as a part of their work as bishops in the church of God is to go beyond—**add** to—the doctrine of Christ and not **aid** in doing God's will. Such an arrangement represents a corruption or perversion of God's plan and is therefore without faith and sinful.

It might appear expedient in the eyes of men to have the same group of elders supervise the work of many congregations, but such would be an "episcopacy" and does not come within the scope of that which God has authorized and is, therefore, without scriptural authority and unlawful. It is contrary to God's arrangement and can never be expedient in accomplishing God's will.

III. In order for a thing to be expedient in the church of God, it must edify (1 Corinthians 10:23-33).

1. Let all things be done unto edifying (1 Corinthians 14:26). If a thing be a matter of choice or expediency—human wisdom or judgment—and its practice tears down and destroys what God would have built up by creating disunity, dissension, and division in the body of Christ, it is sinful and wrong.

If God commands, it must be done in spite of the consequences. If doing the will of God requires it, men have no choice but to obey God (Acts 4:18-20; 5:29). But if it is a non-essential—God having left the choice to human wisdom—and we demand or enforce that which destroys the peace and unity of God's children, we sin. All of the seeming good that we might accomplish by such a course would not overcome the wrong done by it.

IV. In order for a thing to be expedient, it must not offend the conscience of a brother.

1. "Give none offense, neither to the Jews, nor the Gentiles, nor to the church of God" (1 Corinthians 10:32). This rule governs only in matters of expediency—where God has not specified—where the liberty of a choice by human wisdom or judgment has been permitted by the divine will.

   The passage teaches that we are to forego and sacrifice a matter of personal liberty—a non-essential matter—rather than lead a brother to sin by violating his conscience in partaking in that which he believes to be wrong (1 Corinthians 8:7-13).

   If a method of doing the Lord's work is a matter of expediency— God having not legislated but having left the selection of a method to human wisdom and given us the liberty of choice— we cannot force upon the consciences of others those things which our judgment may approve but which are contrary to their understanding and which appear to them to be wrong or sinful without sinning ourselves.

V. We cannot claim an addition to God's word or a substitution for God's way as an expedient.

1. Christ has commanded to teach. He has not specified the method. But he has specified the organization which is to do it— the church—the pillar and ground of truth (Matthew 28:18-20; 1 Timothy 3:15). We have no choice as to organization, for to build another to do the work which Christ established the church to do is to ignore God's arrangement for our own. But we do have a choice as to which method—public or private, entire assembly or class, with or without human aids such as literature, etc.

2. Christ commanded "drink this cup" (1 Corinthians 11:25-28). The cup is the fruit of the vine (Matthew 26:27-29). We have no choice as to the element but we do have a choice as to the number of containers. That is a matter of human wisdom or judgment since Christ did not specify.

3. Christ commanded the saints to assemble (Hebrews 10:25). He did not specify as to how the place of assembly shall be provided, whether the house in which the saints assemble shall be rented, borrowed, or owned. The command implies and includes within its scope some place as essential but whether the congregation is to rent, borrow, or own is a matter of expediency and to be determined by the saints.

4. Instrumental music is not a matter of expediency. There is no authority for it. Nothing the Lord has commanded includes or permits it. It is, therefore, an addition to the Lord's word and will.

    Whether or not we sing out of a book, with the aid of lights, sitting in seats or standing, or what part we shall sing are all matters of expediency left by the Lord to our judgment. All of these would classify as aids, not additions.

5. Christ commanded the church to do the work of ministering (Ephesians 4:12). This includes caring for her own destitute — those who lawfully are the charge of the church (1 Timothy 5:16).

    The organization through which the Lord's church is to do this work has been specified by the Lord. It is the congregation under its own elders (Acts 14:23; Philippians 1:1). The method has not been specified as to (1) place provided, (2) supervision, (3) discipline, (4) necessities to be furnished, etc., but the method has been left to human wisdom and is a matter of expediency. All of these would come under the jurisdiction of the elders of the congregation doing the work. Elders, however, do not have the right to add another organization to the one God has provided or substitute another therefor.

6. The jurisdiction of the elders of a congregation has been fixed by divine authority (Acts 20:28; 1 Peter 5:2). The same men who are elders of a congregation may assume many other duties. They might run a farm, bank, be on a board of directors of some corporation, supervise an intercongregational program of work, etc. But such work would not be within their authority of elders of the Lord's church. When they extend their jurisdiction beyond the membership and work of the "flock which is among you" or the "flock over which the Holy Ghost has made you bishops," they act *ultra vires*—that is, without the scope of their rightful authority and are guilty of perverting the government of the Lord's church. What elders can oversee has been specified in the word of the Lord and is not a matter of expediency.

When is a New Testament Example Binding?

INTRODUCTION

Example is but one method of teaching in the New Testament Scriptures as we have shown in previous lessons (numbers 3 and 4). The issue to be studied in this lesson is whether or not the authority resting in an example in the New Testament church can exclude those methods for which there is neither precept or example. This study is in the field of interpretation—commonly called **hermeneutics**.

When we can find the church practicing a particular thing or method in the New Testament record with evident apostolic approval, no one with any faith would question the correctness of the same practice today under the same or similar circumstances. If there are two or more examples of methods of doing the same thing, then either would be permissible under the same circumstances now, and we would have a choice in the matter based upon expediency. But the question with which we are concerned in this lesson is this: *When there is an example of but one method of doing a thing in the New Testament scriptures, is that one example exclusive of all other methods or practices?*

That the New Testament teaches by example can surely not be questioned by anyone. But how exclusive is the character of such teaching? Can the New Testament bind upon God's people a practice or method to the exclusion of all others by example? If so, how is such exclusiveness to be determined?

I. **The rule of uniformity.**

1. The application of this rule in conversion.

    (1) In every case of conversion recorded in the word of God from the beginning of the gospel on the day of Pentecost, there is no exception to the fact that the conversion was brought about by the preaching, teaching, and learning of the word of God. Without the word, there were no conversions. That uniformity impresses us with the fact that only by the word of God can conversion be affected today.

    (2) In every case of conversion in the New Testament record, we find faith exercised by the man who heard the word of God.

This established the principle that unless faith is planted in the heart by the hearing of the word of God, there can be no conversion. This rule did not vary in all examples.

(3) The fact that every man who accepted the word of God by faith was baptized without delay in New Testament conversions impresses us by the very uniformity of it with the fact that such an act is essential to conversion.

(4) The fact that the Lord's supper was observed by the early church on the first day of the week and only upon the first day of the week is significant. If it established the right to observe the Lord's supper upon the first day, it also established that it can be observed **only** upon the first day, for we have neither precept, example, or inference of observing it any other day. Therefore, every other day is excluded.

2. The application of this rule to the question of church cooperation.

(1) When many churches cooperated with a preacher by supporting him while preaching the gospel, they sent directly to the individual whom they were supporting (2 Corinthians 11:8; Philippians 4:15-18). Philippi sent directly to Paul by their messenger Epaphroditus.

(2) When many churches cooperated with the Jerusalem church by contributing to help meet the needs of the Jerusalem saints, they made up their own funds, selected their own messenger or messengers, and sent it directly to Jerusalem (1 Corinthians 16:1-4; 2 Corinthians 8:16-24).

(3) When Antioch made up a contribution for the brethren in Judea during the famine there, they sent it by the hands of their own messengers—Paul and Barnabas—to the elders of the church in need (Acts 11:27-30).

(4) There is no precept, example, or inference that any church contributed to the work **through** another church. A centralizing of the funds of many churches and the control over them in a sponsoring church is unknown to the New Testament scriptures. There is no variation from the pattern that when a contribution was made by any congregation from its treasury to any work, it was sent, always, directly to the work being done and never through any church as an intermediate agency. There is complete uniformity and no variation at all in the pattern in all New Testament examples of one church contributing to another church.

II. **The rule of unity.** This is sometimes called the law of harmony. It means that each passage of Scripture whether precept or example must be interpreted in the light of whatever and all else God has said on the same theme. Truth is always in harmony with truth. Any example that violates any precept of truth is not an approved example.

1. The rule illustrated or exemplified.

   (1) Divine precept fixes the jurisdiction of the authority of the elders of a congregation as over the "flock over which they have been made bishops" (Acts 20:28), or "the flock which is among you" (1 Peter 5:2).

   (2) When Antioch sent her contribution to aid the brethren in Judea in time of drought, they sent it to the elders.

      a. There were "churches of God which in Judea are in Christ" among the brethren which dwelt in Judea (1 Thessalonians 2:14).

      b. God's order **was** and **is** elders in every church (Acts 14:23).

      c. The contribution sent to the brethren in Judea by the hands of Paul and Barnabas was delivered into the hands of the elders. What elders? Why, the elders among the brethren which dwelt in Judea. Since there were more than one congregation and since each congregation had elders, we are free to conclude that the contribution from Antioch was placed in the hands of the elders of each church that was in need and that distribution among its needy members was made under the supervision of its own elders.

      d. The conclusion reached by some that the Jerusalem elders received the contribution for all the brethren in Judea and distributed it among them is not only without any basis in fact but is clearly out of harmony with the teaching of the Bible elsewhere on the jurisdiction of an eldership.

   (3) The disciples came together to break bread on the first day of the week (Acts 20:7).

      a. This example is in harmony with the precept "This do in remembrance of me" (1 Corinthians 11:24).

      b. The assembly of the disciples to break bread in this example is in harmony with the apostolic instruction in 1 Corinthians 11:20 and Hebrews 10:25.

   c. The inference that this was a practice on the Lord's day as regularly as it came—each week—is in harmony with apostolic teaching that the supper was to be repeatedly observed (1 Corinthians 11:26).

III. **The rule of universal application.** Everything taught in the gospel of Christ is within the realm of possibility in practice for all people in all parts of the world and in every age. The scope of the gospel is worldwide, both in its provisions and in its requirements.

1. Baptism in water for the remission of sins is a demonstration of the universal applicability of the requirements of the gospel. Water is everywhere that there is life. Where there is not enough water for baptizing, men cannot live. Water is in every part of the world.

2. Weekly observance of the Lord's supper on the first day of the week is likewise within the realm of possibility for men.

3. The autonomy and independence of congregations as taught in the Lord's plan for his church means that in every locality where Christians are made throughout the world, the work of the Lord's church can be carried on without any necessary connection with any other part of the people of God in any other part of the world.

IV. **The law of materiality.** Whether a thing is relevant, material, or essential to the teaching or practice of God's will is a most important consideration. Incidental matters are never relevant, material, or competent in determining the will of God. Incidental circumstances need to be separated from divine law in anything taught in God's word.

1. Whether the people on the day of Pentecost were baptized in a natural stream or an artificial pool or reservoir of water in the city of Jerusalem is entirely incidental. The design, action, and results accomplished were exactly the same in any event.

2. Whether the gospel is preached in a temple of worship, by the riverside, or in the jail house is a matter that is neither relevant or material to the conversion of the sinner. The truth preached, believed, and obeyed constituted conversion under any circumstances.

3. Whether Christians assemble under the branches of a tree, in a rented hall, in a private home, or in a building owned by them is a matter of indifference completely. The assembly of the

saints in worship in spirit and truth is the essential whether in Jerusalem or Baghdad (John 4:21-24). Whether the Lord's supper is observed in an upper room, on the third story, or in a house with but one story is entirely immaterial (Matthew 18:20).

4. Whether in the Lord's supper the elements are the unleavened loaf and the fruit of the vine or ice cream and cake is a very material matter. The emblems of his body and blood on the Lord's table were determined by him and are the constituent elements of the supper he ordained. Anything else could not possibly constitute that supper.

5. Whether a congregation has elders or not is material, because unless in due time elders are developed and appointed, God's order has not been respected and followed (Acts 14:23).

6. Whether elders exercise jurisdiction over the congregation in which they have been made elders or in some organization other than that congregation only or many congregations is a very material question as to whether they are exercising scriptural authority in the function of their office (1 Peter 5:2). It simply determines whether they are elders or something else and whether they are exercising proper authority or are usurping authority.

7. Whether congregations maintain an equal relationship to any work in which two or more churches cooperate is very material in determining whether or not they respect the divine order of the autonomy, independence, and equality of New Testament congregations. Whenever two or more congregations combine their funds and centralize the control over "their" work in one congregation and under one eldership, they have violated a very material and essential principle of New Testament church identity—its government.

V. **The law of competence.** In studying any precept or example from New Testament Scriptures, it is important to determine whether or not the evidence obtainable from the divine record is actually competent to support the claim that is made for it. Practices which we are anxious to justify are too often presumed when the evidence of their actual existence in the Scriptures is non-existent.

1. The presumption that the Jerusalem elders took charge of the contribution sent from Antioch for the brethren which dwelt in Judea and distributed that benevolence among the churches in Judea is entirely unsupported. In the example of Acts 11:27-30,

Jerusalem and the Jerusalem elders are not mentioned. We are entitled to presume that the churches in Judea followed the divine order of "elders in every church" (Acts 14:23). In that case, the elders to whom Paul and Barnabas delivered the contribution were the elders among the brethren in Judea. Unless it could be established that only the Jerusalem church had elders, which is entirely without support, then we must conclude that the elders of the various churches in Judea which were in need are the ones referred to in the example.

2. The idea that any New Testament congregation ever made a contribution to any work to be done through another church is pure fiction. There is no example or hint of such a practice in the New Testament. There is no pooling of funds among New Testament churches. In the contribution sent to the Jerusalem saints, each church selected its own messenger to carry the funds to Jerusalem and thus retained control, through their agent, over the funds until they came to rest in Jerusalem where the need existed and the work was to be done (1 Corinthians 16:1-4; 2 Corinthians 8:16-24). Philippi sent directly to Paul by her own messenger—Epaphroditus (Philippians 4:15-18). This is the pattern.

3. There is no testimony of any kind upon which to base the presumption that New Testament churches ever undertook to do their work through any organization other than the congregation under its own elders.

VI. The law of limited application. Every principle of divine law demonstrated in any New Testament example can be correctly applied only to the circumstances or set of facts under which application is made by the Holy Spirit in the word of God. No example or principle applied to all circumstances or conditions. The case to which it is to be applied must be the same fact situation. There must be a case in point.

Examples:

1. Much of the teaching in 1 Corinthians 14 cannot be generally applied for the reason that Paul was dealing with a fact situation that cannot be reproduced today—the proper use of spiritual gifts. The principle to be learned for general application is stated, "Let all things be done unto edifying" and "Let all things be done decently and in order."

2. Many of the things written by Paul concerning the marriage relationship in 1 Corinthians 7 were written "in view of the present distress" and therefore are limited in their application and would be misused if generally applied to all circumstances and situations.

3. The community of property practiced in the Jerusalem church was not intended for general emulation but was practiced only under special circumstances and in a particular situation (Acts 2:45; 4:32).

4. In New Testament Scriptures, one church never contributed to another church unless that church was in need. They did contribute to churches in need (churches of Macedonia, Achaia, and Galatia to Jerusalem). A contribution by one church to another church in need does not justify one church promoting another church out of its money to do a good work. That is not a case in point because the fact situation is not the same.

VII.**The law of exclusion.** When there is no precept, approved example, or necessary inference that includes the practice under consideration, there is no authority for such practice and it is excluded. God's silence rules against it and to engage in such a practice is to add to the law of God. We must not only speak where the Bible speaks but we must be silent where the Bible is silent (2 John 9-11).

The Church and the Christian Individual

INTRODUCTION

The failure to separate what the congregation, as such, can do and what the individual Christian can do in the service of the Lord is the cause of much misunderstanding in the church today.

There are two modern theories advanced: (1) what the Christian individual can do, the church can do, and (2) what the church cannot do, the Christian individual cannot do. These two positions represent two extreme views and are both wrong. Some of the brethren have contended that if the Christian individual can support a school in which the Bible is taught along with secular subjects, then the church can do so out of its treasury. Others have contended that if the church cannot support a school in which the Bible is taught along with secular subjects, then a Christian individual cannot do so. Such misconceptions are based upon the fallacy that whatever the Christian does, the church is doing. It is the purpose of this lesson to emphasize that there are many things which the Christian individual must do in his individual relationships in living the Christian life that the church, as such, cannot engage in scripturally.

I. **What it means to be a Christian.**

1. It means more than simply subscribing to a system of doctrine, though without the truth of God it is impossible to be a Christian (John 8:32).

2. It means more than simply believing. Theoretical religion alone is not enough. To be sure, one must be a believer (Hebrews 11:6; Mark 16:16). But he must have a faith that works by love (Galatians 5:6).

3. It means submission, obedience and conformity to the will of Christ in every relationship in life, in all manner of living (1 Peter 1:13-16; James 1:22-27).

4. It certainly includes being a member of the body of Christ—the church—but it includes more than just church membership.

    (1) One cannot be a Christian—a saved individual—without being a member of the church. God adds the saved to the church (Acts 2:47).

II. The religion of Christ is a way of life embracing every relationship in the life of the Christian individual.

1. It is just as necessary for a Christian to please God and do his will in the home, in the conduct of his business, in his relation to the government, and in his social contact with his fellow man as it is in the church.

2. A man who does not live in his home according to the principles of righteousness, who does not conduct his business according thereto, who does not fulfill his duty before God toward the government under which he lives, or who does not treat his fellow man as a Christian should is not a Christian. It does not matter how faithful he may be in the work of the church or in its worship.

3. The Christian life and duty embraces every relationship in life. It is a twenty-four hour day, seven day each week job and nothing in the life of the individual Christian is exempt from it.

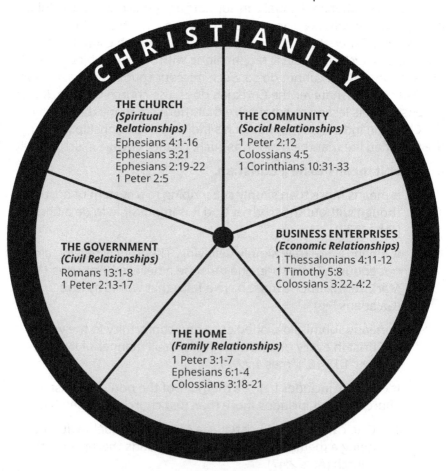

III. Some individual Christian duties that cannot be performed by the church.

1. A Christian is under obligation to make a living for his family. He cannot shun this obligation and put it on the church (1 Timothy 5:8, 16).

2. A Christian is under obligation to bring his children up in the nurture and admonition of the Lord. While it is certainly right for the church to teach anybody, child or adult, whenever it has the opportunity, the church cannot take over the task of rearing our children for us (Ephesians 6:4).

3. The Christian individual is to engage in some sort of gainful occupation to provide for himself, those who have the right to depend upon him, and in order to be able to give, but the church cannot engage in business or economic enterprise (1 Thessalonians 4:11; 1 Timothy 5:8; 2 Thessalonians 3:10).

4. The Christian is subject to the government under which he lives as a citizen, but the church is not a political medium and has no relation to the civil government (1 Peter 2:13; Romans 13:1-8).

5. The Christian individual has obligations to his community, to the people with whom he works, among whom he lives, and with whom he associates that is no part of the work of the Lord's church in any sense (Romans 12:14-21).

IV. Some duties assigned both to the Christian individual and the church.

1. In some work, the individual Christian is to function both in his individual capacity and as a member of the church (congregation) in doing God's will.

    (1) **Teaching.** In Acts 11, we have an example of individuals planting Christianity in Antioch (verse 20) by preaching the word and also of the church in Jerusalem sending out Barnabas to assist in the work of preaching the word there (verses 22-24).

    (2) **Benevolence** is in some instances an individual obligation and in some instances it is chargeable to the church (1 Timothy 5:16).

2. In no instance does the discharge of individual Christian duty conflict with one's duty to God in the church. We should do both to the best of our ability realizing that we have many duties to discharge as individuals that cannot be performed by the church,

as such, and there are duties that must be discharged in the church that cannot be discharged through any other relationship.

V. Each Christian individual is responsible to God for doing his part of whatever God has made the church responsible for in his service.

1. The church is to be built up by that which each member supplies (Ephesians 4:16).

2. The body has many members. There is but one body (1 Corinthians 12:12). Every member has its function to perform and is needed (1 Corinthians 12:14-26). All are to function in their respective places and according to their ability in doing the work of the church (Romans 12:4-8). The arrangement in the body is of God (1 Corinthians 12:18).

3. The Corinthian church had an obligation for which they had committed themselves in helping the Jerusalem saints (2 Corinthians 8:10-11; 9:5). That "aforepromised bounty" was to be made up by each one contributing his proportionate part on the first day of the week (1 Corinthians 16:1-4). So it is always in financing the work of the Lord's church.

4. Each member is responsible for maintaining peace and harmony in accordance with God's will in the congregation (Ephesians 4:1-3).

5. Each member of the body is responsible for its purity (Ephesians 4:17; 5:21).

CONCLUSION

Thus, we can see that while the responsibility for making the church what God wants it to be and for accomplishing the purposes of God through it rests upon the individual member—and he is obligated to do his part, determined by his ability, of whatever God wants the church to do and for making his efforts blend in with the efforts of other members of the body—his obligations in the work of the church are not all of the personal responsibility which rests upon him. He is responsible for doing the will of God in all of the relationships of his life. What God has given the church to do must be done through the church, and what God has given the individual Christian to do as an individual he must do as such and cannot avoid his personal duty by trying to let the church perform it in his stead. Let the church be the church and let the church do the work of the church.

The Autonomy of the Local Church

INTRODUCTION

Autonomy means self-government. God gave to the congregation the right of self-government. Each local church is subject to Christ and his authority alone. This right of self-government depends in its actual application upon two other scriptural principles characteristic of each church of Christ: the principle of the independence of each church and the equality of all the churches of Christ.

I. Christ gave his church a congregational form of government.

1. "Elders in every church" (Acts 14:23). These elders were within the local church and ruled over its affairs in harmony with the will of Christ (Philippians 1:1; Acts 20:28; 1 Peter 5:1-4; Hebrews 13:17).

2. These elders, bishops, or pastors over each local church had jurisdiction only over the flock among them or over which they had been made bishops. They could extend it no further by divine authority (Acts 20:28; 1 Peter 5:2).

3. This divine arrangement specified by the authority of Christ through his apostles excluded all other organizations or forms of government for directing or overseeing the affairs of the churches of Christ. They had nothing larger than the local church and nothing smaller than the local church.

    (1) The thing specifically authorized always excludes everything else in the same order or class (see Lesson 3, Paragraph V, Generic and Specific Authority). Hence, the congregation being the only arrangement which Christ has authorized for the government of his church and the direction of its function, it excludes all others. Any human arrangement provided for the oversight and the government of the work of the church of the Lord is not an **aid** in doing its work but is rather an **addition** or substitution to the word of the Lord (see Lesson 4, Paragraph V).

II. The congregation was the only medium through which the New Testament church functioned in the performance of its mission.

1. Each congregation did its own work under the supervision of its own elders.

(1) The local church sent out preachers (Acts 11:22).

(2) The local church supported preachers laboring in new fields (Philippians 4:15-18; 1:4-7).

(3) The local church made up its own funds for benevolent work (1 Corinthians 16:1-3; Acts 11:27-30).

(4) The local church selected and sent its own messengers with its funds for the work to be done (1 Corinthians 16:1-4; 2 Corinthians 8:4-6, 16-21).

(5) The messenger of the local church making the contribution delivered the contribution entrusted to him to the elders of the congregations where the relief was needed (Acts 11:30).

2. There is nothing which God has ordained that the church should do which cannot be carried out through the organization which God has given it—the congregation.

3. There is no attribute of the church as the body of Christ which the local church does not possess. The congregation built after the divine pattern is perfect and complete.

III. The congregation was the only medium through which the Christians of the New Testament age functioned in accomplishing the mission which the Lord assigned his church.

1. Paul associated himself with the congregation at Jerusalem (Acts 9:26).

2. Fellowship with the church in its work necessitates working in conjunction with other members of the congregation (Romans 12:4-5). Those added together in Jerusalem to constitute the body of the saved continued steadfastly in fellowship one with another (Acts 2:42).

3. Each congregation has the right to refuse fellowship in its work and worship to any unworthy individual (1 Corinthians 5:1-13; 2 Thessalonians 3:6-7, 14-15).

4. The congregations of the New Testament came together on the Lord's day to worship (Acts 20:7; 1 Corinthians 11:17-22). Christians were commanded not to forsake the assembly (Hebrews 10:25). The church a spiritual house in which to offer up spiritual sacrifices (1 Peter 2:5).

5. Christians were admonished to work together, be at peace, and submit themselves to the authority of Christ as members of the congregation and under the elders of that congregation of which they were a part (1 Thessalonians 5:11-14).

6. Individual members of the congregation were held responsible for enabling the congregation to do its work (Ephesians 4:16; 2 Corinthians 9:5-7).

IV. **There were no inter-congregational alliances among the New Testament churches but each church did its own work under the direction of its own elders.**

1. The Jerusalem congregation took care of its own needy within the framework of the congregation itself (Acts 2:44-45; 4:32-37).

   (1) "Wherefore look ye out among you seven men of honest report, full of the Holy Ghost and wisdom, whom we may appoint over this business" (Acts 6:3). Thus from among their own members were men selected to attend to the care of the needy in this congregation.

2. Several churches supported Paul while he preached at Corinth (2 Corinthians 11:8). Each church sent directly to Paul by its own messenger as did Philippi (Philippians 4:14-18). There is no indication in the divine record of it being done any other way.

3. The churches of Macedonia, Achaia, and Galatia sent to the relief of the poor saints at Jerusalem when the need was so great that the Jerusalem congregation could not meet it (Romans 15:25-27, 31). This benevolence was sent to Jerusalem (1 Corinthians 16:3). It was sent by the messenger (individual) selected or chosen by each church (1 Corinthians 16:3-4; 2 Corinthians 8:16-24). There was no pooling of funds in this case and no combining funds under centralized control existed in New Testament days. The funds were administered where they were sent by the elders of the church (Acts 11:30).

V. **No church became the agent of another church in the New Testament day.**

1. All churches bore an equal relationship to whatever work they cooperated in doing. There were no "sponsoring churches" and "contributing churches." No congregation received and forwarded funds for another. Such was not a New Testament practice and cannot be found in New Testament scriptures. However harmless it may seem, such a practice creates an inequality that is wrong and which inevitably leads, if practiced, to the destruction of autonomy.

2. Agency cannot exist without subordination. Whenever one church becomes the agent of another church, one is subordinated to the other, either the church contributing tells the church receiving what to do or the receiving church is authorized to act for the contributing church. Equality cannot exist either way. That such is voluntary does not mean that autonomy cannot be surrendered voluntarily just the same as any other liberty or right.

3. There were no congregations that promoted themselves into a "brotherhood agency" for doing any work for many churches and then brought pressure to bear through their propaganda and by their agents to raise the money such work necessitated.

4. It is sometimes argued that in 2 Corinthians 11:7-8; Philippians 2:25; and 4:14-18 all the churches contributing to Paul's support sent to Philippi, which, as a sponsoring church, sent on to Paul. This contention is based on the statement, "No church communicated with me as concerning giving and receiving but ye only," (Philippians 4:15). The word is *koinoneo* translated in the King James "communicated" in Philippians 4:15 and Galatians 6:6. The same form of the word occurs in Romans 12:13, 15:27; 1 Timothy 5:22; Hebrews 2:14; 1 Peter 4:13; and 2 John 11 and is translated "distributing" and "partaking." The *koinonia* is more often translated as "fellowship" and is so rendered in the American Standard edition in Philippians 4:15.

The expression "as concerning giving and receiving" is paraphrased by McKnight as follows: "No church communicated with me in the matter of giving and of my receiving money from them, but ye only."

If Philippi received from other churches and fowarded the funds to Paul—simply keeping books for Paul—in the manner of a "sponsoring church" as some of our modern(-istic) scholars contend today, then the contributing churches had no fellowship with Paul in supplying his needs for such was true only of Philippi. To see the point illustrated, consult the following chart:

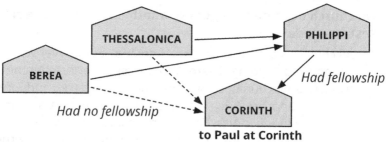

CONCLUSION

High pressure promotion programs sponsored by one church and financed by money solicited from all the churches, sponsoring arrangements for cooperation among churches, and one church acting as the agency through which many churches do their work will all eventually lead to the complete surrender of autonomy, independence, and equality and therefore to the destruction of congregational government. Romanism is this sort of thing developed to its ultimate conclusion.

The Extent and Limitations of the Authority of Elders

INTRODUCTION

This lesson is essential in understanding the divine provisions for the government of the church of the Lord. In divine affairs, all authority inheres in God, and in the Christian dispensation, all authority has been given into the hands of Christ. He is the head over all things to the church, which is his body (Ephesians 1:22-23). No one is authorized to do anything in the church except by him.

I.   **Elders in the Lord's church have no legislative authority.**

1.   They cannot make laws but can function only as they are authorized to do by the Lord. Christ alone has legislative authority. "There is one lawgiver" (James 4:12).

2.   Truth is determined by the word of God and is settled in Heaven forever (Psalm 119:89). All men must determine what is truth by the same standard (John 17:17). All have equal access to it.

3.   Elders, then, are not to make creeds for Christians to believe, teach, or live by. Their rule is within the realm of faith, in matters of expediency, within the realm of things authorized by the Lord.

 (1) They are not lords. Even in the realm of judgment, they are to do the will of the Lord and not their own. Nor are they to use their office as a means of enforcing their own prejudices and preferences to the disregard of the good and rights of the flock over which they rule (1 Peter 5:1-4; James 4:11).

   a. Contrast Diotrephes and Demetrius (3 John 9-12).

II. **Elders are to be obeyed as overseers (bishops) and shepherds (pastors) that watch for our souls (Hebrews 13:17; 1 Thessalonians 5:12-13).**

1.   To refuse to be submissive to the rule of elders in the congregation as long as they rule in harmony with the will of the Lord is to rebel against the authority of Christ. But when elders become lords over God's heritage, depart from the faith, or usurp power and authority which God never gave them, no Christian should submit to them. We must obey God rather than men, no matter what position of authority they have (Acts 5:29).

(1) A Christian woman is to submit to her husband only "in the Lord" (Ephesians 5:22).

(2) Children are to obey their parents "in the Lord" (Ephesians 6:1-3).

(3) Christian citizens are to obey laws of the land as long as they do not conflict with the laws of God (Acts 5:29).

(4) Members of a congregation are to obey the elders of that congregation as long as they do the will of Christ and act by his authority (1 Peter 5:1-4; 1 Timothy 5:17-20).

III. Elders have the oversight of all matters within the local congregation.

1. The word "bishop" (*episkopos*) means "overseer."

2. Elders are responsible for upholding the word of the Lord (Acts 20:28-32).

   (1) They must be able to convince the "gainsayer" (Titus 1:9).

   (2) They must know the truth, be "apt to teach" (1 Timothy 3:2), able to meet and turn back false doctrine and false teachers (Titus 1:9-14), and thus keep the church from apostasy (Acts 20:28-31).

3. This in no sense gives any elders the right to write their own sentiments, preferences, judgments, or will into a creed and bind it upon preachers, teachers, or a congregation. Let them be able to meet any error with truth and thus turn away false teaching and teachers. They have no right to make any demand on anyone that they are not able to establish by the word of the Lord.

4. The Scriptures nowhere restrict the oversight of the elders to "spiritual matters" while deacons oversee and control the financial and material affairs of a congregation.

   (1) There is nothing in the text to justify the conclusion that the seven appointed in the Jerusalem congregation constituted regular deacons in that church (Acts 6:1-4). They were appointed for but one service—"wait on tables"—and when the need no longer existed for such service their work ended.

   (2) Deacons are specially qualified and appointed servants subject to elders as are all other Christians. The oversight of elders includes their work as it does the work of all others in the flock without restriction as to scope (1 Peter 5:2; Acts 20:28; Philippians 1:1).

IV. Elders are "congregational" and not "universal" officers (Philippians 1:1).

1. They are to take "oversight of the flock of God which is among you" (1 Peter 5:12).

2. They are to "take heed to the flock over which the Holy Ghost hath made you overseers" (Acts 20:28).

3. They can exercise discipline only within the congregation where they are elders (1 Corinthians 5:1-5; 2 Thessalonians 3:6). These instructions were given to a local church. In no place in New Testament scriptures did God give elders any jurisdiction over members of another congregation. They are responsible only for those whom they "rule" (Hebrews 13:17).

4. They can be disciplined by those whom they rule (1 Timothy 5:19-21).

5. Contrary to the Catholic idea, elders have no right to interfere with or seek to control or exercise authority over the personal, private affairs of any Christian's home, business, social activities, or political and civil affairs. If a Christian—a member of the congregation over which they are overseers—is not living in harmony with the will of the Lord in any of these relationships, they have the obligation to teach, exhort, admonish, etc. and if he will not walk uprightly, they can refuse him fellowship in the congregation, but that is the end of their authority.

6. When benevolence was sent by the disciples at Antioch through Paul and Barnabas as messengers to the "brethren which dwelt in Judea" (Acts 11:27-30) they delivered it into the hands of the elders for distribution. There is no variation from this example for the distribution of benevolence among brethren. It was a congregational function, within the congregation, and was therefore under the supervision of the overseers of the congregation, the elders. There is no indication of any activity within any New Testament congregation that was an exception to this rule. There is no such thing as a "diocesan" eldership in the church of the Lord. Elders ruled over only one congregation and over all of the members and work of that congregation.

7. The undisputed testimony of all religious historians shows that the apostasy in New Testament days began by elders extending their authority beyond the limits prescribed by the word of the Lord. This is an ever-present danger.

V. Elders have no scriptural right to delegate their authority to the elders of another congregation.

1. This would permit the centralizing of power over many churches in the hands of one eldership and destroy congregational government, thus defeating God's arrangement. There is no scriptural authority for such a delegation of responsibility.

2. The very nature of the office and the obligations involved in it confine its function to a relationship between those who are ruled and those who rule over them. The elders are to "watch for their souls as they that shall give account unto God" (Hebrews 13:17). Since it is a duty for which they are responsible to God, they cannot avoid it by delegating it to others and please God.

3. The "oversight of the flock of God which is among you" precludes any oversight by any shepherd or elder which is not among the flock or congregation (1 Timothy 5:17-20; 1 Peter 5:1-4).

4. Just as God holds members of a congregation responsible for "obeying them that rule over you" so God holds them that rule over the flock, the elders, responsible for ruling over each Christian who is obligated to obey them and for the oversight of the work of that flock over which he has been made bishop or elder (Acts 20:20-32; 1 Peter 5:1-4). This responsibility the elders of one congregation cannot rightfully delegate even voluntarily to the elders of another congregation nor can they permit another eldership to usurp it.

VI. The efficient and proper functioning of each congregation through its every member and in all of its work is then the responsibility of the eldership of each local church and cannot be delegated by them to another.

1. One church in the New Testament contributed to another church to enable it to meet its own obligation and do its own work in the time of need, but one church cannot scripturally yield to another church the responsibility and obligation of overseeing its own work and doing the work for which God has made each congregation responsible to the extent of its ability (1 Corinthians 16:1-4; Acts 11:27-30).

2. The eldership of one congregation has as much scriptural authority to oversee the worship, edification, and discipline of another congregation as they have to oversee the benevolence or evangelistic program of another congregation. If they can oversee the distribution of a part of the funds of another church

in any of its work, then they can oversee the distribution of all of its funds for all of its work.

3. If the eldership can scripturally oversee the spending of funds contributed by many churches, by what right or reason can that same eldership be precluded from teaching, exhorting, reproving the members of those contributing congregations concerning their duty in giving the funds?

VII. **God gave elders the "oversight" only of matters pertaining to a congregation and its function.**

1. When elders become directors, a board of trustees, or officers in any other arrangement or organization than the church they are acting in another capacity than as elders of the congregation. God did not intend them to oversee anything but the church.

2. When elders take the oversight of any program of work such as banking, farming, dairying, real estate, secular education, or anything of the sort outside of the work of the Lord's church, they exercise oversight in another capacity than elders and exercise authority in such work that they did not receive from the Lord.

3. To be directors of something besides the church and over work which is not within the scope of the mission of the Lord's church then cannot be a part of the work of overseeing the flock of God.

CONCLUSION

When any eldership becomes ambitious to promote a work, however good it may seem to them, they must remember that they have the right under the Lord to obligate, teach, exhort, discipline, and oversee only the members of the flock over which they have been made bishops by the Holy Spirit and they have only the right from the Lord to take the oversight of the flock of God and its function and nothing else. When they exercise any other authority or right, as elders, they have perverted the office and authority of elders as it is set forth by the Lord in his word.

How New Testament Congregations Cooperated

INTRODUCTION

According to *Webster's New International Dictionary* (The Merriam Series) "cooperation" means: "1. Act of cooperating; joint operation; concurrent effort or labor." By scriptural cooperation between congregations the issue is raised whether or not New Testament churches acted **jointly** or **concurrently**. That is, did two or more congregations combine or pool their funds and centralize their control under one agency as a means of cooperation or did they act independently and concurrently with each other in their efforts to accomplish the same goal? Only a careful study of New Testament Scriptures can give us the true answer to these issues.

I. **One church helped other churches in time of emergency by contributing to their needs (Acts 11:27-30).**

1. The disciples (church) in Antioch contributed to needs of brethren in Judea in time of famine.

2. This incident occurred about A.D. 45. Claudius Caesar began to reign in 41 and Josephus the Jewish historian tells us of a severe famine which began about the fourth year of his reign.

3. This incident is not to be confused with the need of the poor saints in Jerusalem (1 Corinthians 16:1-4; Romans 15:25-28; 2 Corinthians 8, 9) for that was many years later. The first Corinthian letter was written about A.D. 57 or 58.

4. How did Antioch carry out the cooperation with these brethren in Judea?

    (1) The money was raised by the disciples in Antioch contributing "every man according to his ability." Since the disciples in Antioch constituted the church in Antioch and since they contributed into a common fund (joint action) it is only reasonable to conclude that this was congregational activity. 1 Corinthians 16:1-2 later gave specific authorization for the method of raising such a fund in a congregation.

    (2) Paul and Barnabas were chosen by these disciples as messengers to take this fund to the brethren which dwelt in Judea.

(3) These funds were delivered into the hands of the elders among the brethren in Judea.

    a. Since elders were congregational officers (Acts 14:23);

    b. And since the brethren in Judea constituted several congregations (1 Thessalonians 2:14; Galatians 1:22);

    c. We conclude that the funds were delivered by the messengers into the hands of the elders of every congregation where there was a need and they distributed them.

    d. There is no reason to conclude or basis upon which to even presume that the elders in this passage meant the elders in Jerusalem only.

        (a) Unless Jerusalem only had elders and no evidence to that effect can be found. Besides, if we are to presume, the presumption would be that all congregations in Judea had elders since that is God's established order for a congregation (Acts 14:23).

        (b) Then too, if Jerusalem elders took charge of the distribution of funds among all the congregations of Judea, they most certainly acted outside of their own congregation and over the other congregations in which they made this distribution. That would authorize "diocesan" elders—elders in a territory over many churches—which is an "episcopacy" like denominations have and which cannot be justified in the word of God.

The Principle Illustrated: One Church Sends to Many—How?

Not This...

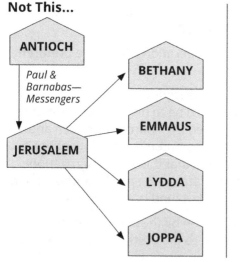

But This (Acts 11:27-30)

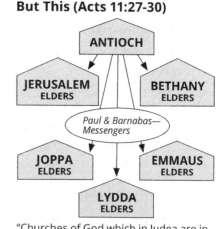

"Churches of God which in Judea are in Christ Jesus" (1 Thessalonians 2:14).
"Elders in every church" (Acts 14:23).

II. Congregations of Galatia, Macedonia, and Achaia cooperated (acted concurrently) in meeting the needs of Jerusalem church (Romans 15:25-28; 1 Corinthians 16:1-4; 2 Corinthians 8, 9).

1. We do not know what brought about this need. It may have been the persecution and dispersion that had impoverished them or in selling their houses and their lands to meet the early crisis in the church they may have become destitute. The famine some years later could have contributed to it. But whatever the cause, there were so many destitute saints in Jerusalem that the church there could not meet the need. There is certainly no record to indicate that these needy saints were not members of the Jerusalem church nor is there the slightest indication that they had gone out and gathered up destitute saints from all over Judea and other provinces in order to do this work and that they thereby had "created" the need that existed among them.

   (1) The primary responsibility is that a congregation shall care for its own. This Jerusalem was obligated to do. Hence the work to be done was the work of the Jerusalem church. But it was greater than the church there alone could meet.

2. Gentile churches to whom the Gospel had gone out from Jerusalem saints were called upon to reciprocate by sending to their need (Romans 15:25-27).

3. This Galatia, Macedonia, and Achaia did upon instruction from Paul (1 Corinthians 16:1-4; 2 Corinthians 8, 9).

4. Macedonian brethren gave beyond their ability because of their deep consecration upon their own accord and besought Paul to accept this gift in behalf of the saints in Jerusalem (2 Corinthians 8:1-5).

5. The Corinthian brethren had been the first to make a "beginning a year ago" when they had been stirred to do so by Titus (2 Corinthians 8:6-10).

6. Paul exhorted Titus to go ahead of the rest into Achaia, taking with him the "brother whose praise is in the gospel throughout all the churches" (2 Corinthians 8:18) and "our brother, whom we have oftentimes proved diligent in many things" (2 Corinthians 8:22). This exhortation Titus accepted (2 Corinthians 8:16-17). These other brethren had been chosen of the churches to travel with Paul, Titus, and others as their messengers to take their contribution to Jerusalem (2 Corinthians 8:19-23). Paul and not the churches, however, had sent them beforehand into Achaia (2 Corinthians 8:18, 22), and he wrote the Corinthian brethren

urging that with the help and encouragement of these brethren they get their "aforepromised bounty" ready so that his boasting of their readiness be not in vain (2 Corinthians 9:1-5). They thus went ahead of Paul into Achaia to help them get their contribution ready for Paul's coming.

7. Each church raised its own fund by each of its members contributing their proportionate part on the first day of the week (1 Corinthians 16:1-2).

   (1) Upon this day the saints assembled to break bread (Acts 20:7).

   (2) By contributing when they had come together they got the money together in a common fund and obviated the necessity of gathering it up when the time came to send it.

8. Each church, acting independently, chose its own messenger to entrust with its contribution that it might be taken to Jerusalem (1 Corinthians 16:1-4; 2 Corinthians 8:19, 23).

   (1) Several churches may have approved the same messenger but each church had the responsibility and right of choosing its own (1 Corinthians 16:3).

   (2) There is not the slightest indication of a convention of many churches in which these messengers were elected in joint action. Such would constitute a denominational convention or association machinery and procedure of first rank.

   (3) If these men had been chosen by churches convened to take collective action, they would have constituted a separate organic body and would have performed a function the local church could not perform. Thus would be justified a convention, association, or conference to function over the churches and for them distributing benevolence among the members of the Jerusalem congregation with denominational machinery, power, and control. No man can read this into the Scriptures and yet condemn the Methodist Conference and the Baptist associations and conventions. Such is not recorded or even hinted in the divine record.

   (4) Each church entrusted their contribution to their own selected agent or messenger and he became responsible to them and the Lord for faithfully delivering it to Jerusalem. There is not the slightest hint of these separate contributions losing their identity in a pooled or combined fund. Such is imagined by some and has no basis in the scriptural record.

This was concurrent action but independent action by each church and this is the pattern of cooperation between congregations in New Testament days.

(5) No church sent its money through another church. There was no intermediate or sponsoring church to receive or forward the funds. All the contributing churches who had a part in this fellowship for Jerusalem sustained an equal relationship to the work being done. Jerusalem alone bore a different relationship and that was because it was among their own members that the need existed which was greater than they could relieve by themselves; it was therefore their own work. Neither was it a created need or a promoted work which they had undertaken and which they were not able to discharge and therefore had to resort to promoting other congregations out of their money in order to do. Nothing in the divine record justifies such a practice. It is entirely foreign to New Testament Scriptures.

9. In the absence of any information to the contrary, we are forced to conclude that when these messengers, including Paul, brought these funds from these various churches to Jerusalem they did as Paul and Barnabas had previously done and delivered it into the hands of the elders of the church (Acts 11:27-30). No change in procedure in this case is even hinted.

The Principle Illustrated: Many Churches Send to One—How?

Not This...

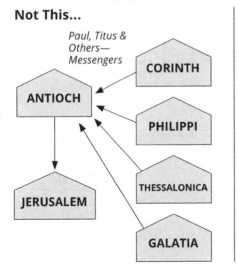

But This (1 Corinthians 16:1-2; 2 Corinthians 8, 9)

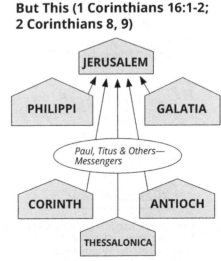

II. Churches cooperated in supporting Paul while he labored to plant the kingdom in Corinth.

1. He took wages from other churches (2 Corinthians 11:8).

2. Philippi was among the churches that supported him (Philippians 1:3-5; 4:10-18).

3. In the example of the Philippian church, we learn how these funds were sent to Paul (Philippians 4:15-18). They sent directly to Paul by their individual messenger, Epaphroditus (Philippians 2:25). There is the New Testament pattern. It authorizes only the direct method and excludes the indirect method. In every instance the contributing church sent directly and never through another church.

    In both evangelism and benevolence, the local church raised its funds, selected its messenger, and sent directly to the work being done. Where is the passage setting forth either precept, example, or inference that any New Testament church ever sent a contribution through another church to be forwarded to the work being done?

    Where is the precept, example, or inference in a passage of Scripture authorizing many churches to pool their funds, combining them, and centralizing their control under one eldership for the purpose of promoting a good work?

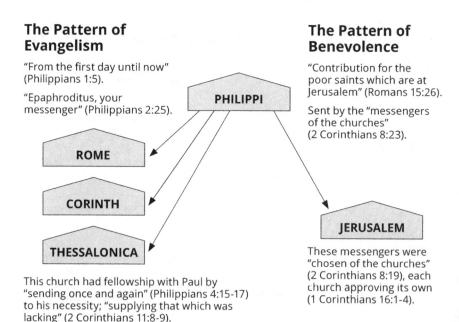

The Pattern of Evangelism

"From the first day until now" (Philippians 1:5).

"Epaphroditus, your messenger" (Philippians 2:25).

This church had fellowship with Paul by "sending once and again" (Philippians 4:15-17) to his necessity; "supplying that which was lacking" (2 Corinthians 11:8-9).

The Pattern of Benevolence

"Contribution for the poor saints which are at Jerusalem" (Romans 15:26).

Sent by the "messengers of the churches" (2 Corinthians 8:23).

These messengers were "chosen of the churches" (2 Corinthians 8:19), each church approving its own (1 Corinthians 16:1-4).

CONCLUSION

Thus New Testament Scriptures furnish us a complete pattern for congregational cooperation:

1. Churches helped each other in time of emergency by contributing directly to the church in need that the need might be supplied and that there might be freedom from want (equality with respect to want) (2 Corinthians 8:13-15).

2. Many churches contributed to one church when it was unable to care for its own.

3. Each church made up its own "bounty," selected its own individual messenger, and sent to the elders of the needy church.

4. Churches sent by their own messenger directly to the support of a preacher.

5. Individuals, not churches, served as messengers of the churches.

6. This service consisted of being entrusted with the funds of the church appointing them until it was delivered to the preacher or elders where it was to be used.

7. The only time any church contributed out of its treasury to another church was when that church was in "want" and in order to make them "free from want."

8. The practice of a church promoting a "good work" and soliciting funds from other churches to pay for it is unknown to the New Testament. *Where is the passage?*

9. The practice of one church sponsoring a work and many churches combining their funds and centralizing the control over those funds in one church and under one eldership cannot be found in the Scriptures and hence has no divine authority but is a perversion of God's plan. *Where is the passage?*

10. The denominational practice of building and maintaining an outside human organization as a means of congregational cooperation is certainly not authorized in the Scriptures and must be therefore sinful. *Where is the passage giving churches of Christ such right?*

The Church and Human Organizations

INTRODUCTION

In this lesson, we are not dealing with method, arrangement, or systematic procedure within the scope of divine authority but rather with other organizations than the church—organizations without and apart from the church—other bodies designed and established by the will and wisdom of men and controlled by human authority to do the work of the church.

"An organization is a body of persons formed into a whole, consisting of independent and coordinated parts, especially for harmonious or united action. A human organization would be such a body formed by man, governed by man, apart from divine origin or authority" (Homer Hailey, *Special Issue Gospel Guardian*, May 3-10, 1956, p. 22).

Can the churches of Christ establish such organizations and maintain them as a means of cooperating in doing any of their work?

I.   **The church of the Lord contrasted with human organizations.**

   1.   The church is a divine organization for the reason that:

      (1)   It was designed by the wisdom of God.

      (2)   It was built by the Lord in fulfillment of God's eternal purpose (Ephesians 3:10-11).

      (3)   It is God's habitation or dwelling place through the Holy Spirit (Ephesians 2:19-22; 1 Corinthians 3:16-17).

      (4)   It is made up of saved men and women redeemed by the blood of Christ and added together by God (Acts 2:47; 20:28; 1 Corinthians 1:2; Ephesians 5:25-27).

      (5)   It is built upon a divine foundation (Matthew 16:16-19; Isaiah 28:14-18; 1 Peter 2:6; 1 Corinthians 3:11).

      (6)   It is ruled by divine authority. Christ is the head over all things to the church (Ephesians 1:22-23).

      (7)   It recognizes the New Testament of which he is mediator as the only rule of faith and practice. Its by-laws are the Scriptures (Hebrews 9:15-17; 10:9-10, 19-22).

(8) It has a divine plan or arrangement (Ephesians 4:11-12; 1 Corinthians 12:18-28).

(9) It has been given a divine mission to accomplish—the purposes of God for which it was designed (Ephesians 4:11-12; 3:10; Colossians 1:23-28; 1 Timothy 2:4; 1 Peter 2:5-10).

(10) The church awaits with hope her final destiny according to God's promises (Colossians 1:27; 1 Peter 1:3-5; 2 Thessalonians 1:10).

2. No human organization possesses any of the above characteristics.

II. God gave his church organic form (organization) to govern in its function.

1. Just as God did not leave the world without form and void but gave to it system and order in his work of creation by natural laws (Genesis 1), so God has not left his church "without form and void" but has given to it a system and order through spiritual laws (1 Corinthians 12:18-29; Ephesians 4:11-12; Matthew 28:18; Ephesians 1:19-23).

2. There is one divine arrangement for the church of God (Ephesians 4:4; 1 Corinthians 12:20, 27; Romans 12:3-8).

3. The local church—congregation—is the only organization or government God gave to his church—each congregation subject to the will of Christ (Philippians 1:1; Acts 14:23; Titus 1:5; 1 Peter 5:1-4).

4. The line of distinction has been drawn by the divine will between that which is human in origin and that which is divine whether in matters of faith, worship, or organization.

    (1) Contrast the difference between what men say and that revealed "not by flesh and blood" but by the "Father in heaven" (Matthew 16:13-20). Here is the dividing line between truth and error in teaching.

    (2) Human innovations established by the doctrines and commandments of men in matters of worship make it vain in God's sight (Matthew 15:1-14). Here is the dividing line between true and vain worship.

    (3) Contrast practices of human origin with practices or ways originating with God (Matthew 21:23-27). Here is the difference between the human and divine will, between the ways of man and the ways of God.

(4)   In this first tabernacle, priests accomplished the service of God (Hebrews 9:6).

(5)   We now have a "tabernacle which the Lord has pitched and not man" (Hebrews 8:1-6).

5.   Our building for God must be according to the divine pattern (Psalm 127:1; 1 Corinthians 3:10-11).

6.   This principle is taught through the tabernacle as a type.

(1)   God gave the pattern for the tabernacle and charged Moses to follow it (Exodus 25; Hebrews 8:1-6).

(2)   This tabernacle was a pattern of heavenly things (Hebrews 9:8-9, 23).

(3)   The shadow purged by the blood of animals (Hebrews 9:21-22).

(4)   "Christ being come...by a more perfect tabernacle not made with hands, not of this building" (Hebrews 9:11).

(5)   This true tabernacle purged by the blood of Christ (Hebrews 10:19-22).

As strictly as God charged Moses to follow the pattern and as plainly as we have this principle applied to the church today, it is unthinkable that God did not give order, arrangement, and form to this more perfect tabernacle or that he left men the liberty of substituting their own arrangement for that which God gave or adding thereto. Read Hebrews 2:1-4; 10:25-31; 12:22-29. We cannot conclude that we have greater liberty under the new covenant when it comes to following God's ways and doing his will.

7.   The pattern of doctrine, worship, and work of the church is the same in all congregations (2 Timothy 1:13; 1 Corinthians 7:17; 4:16-17; 16:1-2; Acts 14:23; Philippians 4:9).

III. No New Testament church ever built and maintained any human organization as a means of doing any of its work.

1.   The Lord never gave the church authority to build anything but the church.

(1)   To illustrate:
Federal government . . . Post office department
State government . . . . . Highway department
Masonic lodge. . . . . Old folks homes
Catholic church. . . . . . . Orphan homes
Church of Christ . . . . Benevolent organizations

Brother Guy N. Woods in the debate at Indianapolis, Indiana in January, 1956 used a chart similar to the above to contend that all of the institutions on the left side of the chart build and maintain the organizations on the right side of the chart and none of them in any sense rival or compete with the institution that establishes them. Brother Porter showed that such logic would justify the churches of Christ building missionary societies as well as benevolent societies, because the Catholic Church builds and maintains missionary societies that do not conflict or compete with it.

The basic fallacy of Brother Woods' argument is in the fact that legislative authority is inherent in all of these organizations to build whatever they please but it is not so in the church of God. Jesus Christ is the head over his church, and it has no right to build anything that he has not authorized it to build (Ephesians 5:22-24).

2. When the church today preaches the same gospel preached by the church in the New Testament times, it will build only the church as it did then, free from all human institutions and arrangements. There is no trace of their existence in New Testament Scriptures to do any work of the church and therefore there is no authority for them now.

IV. **Congregations in New Testament Scriptures did all of their work and fulfilled their God-given mission without any human organizations.**

1. Each church had its own organization through which to function (Philippians 1:1).

2. Each congregation raised its own funds by the contributions of its members (1 Corinthians 16:1-2).

3. Each congregation supported evangelists to preach the gospel throughout the world according to its ability as the Lord ordained (1 Corinthians 9:14; Philippians 2:12-15; 2 Corinthians 11:8; 1 Thessalonians 1:5-8).

    (1) In every instance recorded of Paul's receiving this help, it was sent directly to him (2 Corinthians 11:8-9; Philippians 1:5; 2:25; 4:18).

4. Congregations sent out preachers to strengthen, edify, and help weak churches (Acts 11:22-24).

5. Congregations provided for their own needy (Acts 2:44-45; 4:32-35; 6:1-6).

6. Congregations cooperated with other congregations who had a greater need among their own members than they could supply by sending contributions to the elders of such church through their own selected messengers (Romans 15:25-28; 1 Corinthians 16:1-4; 2 Corinthians 8, 9).

7. Each congregation was edified through that strength supplied by its own members (Ephesians 4:14-16; 1 Corinthians 14:26; 12:22-27).

   Note: Thus each congregation carried on its own work through the organization God gave it. There is not an instance in the Scriptures where churches of Christ ever used any human organization as a medium through which to function in doing its work. It would be interesting for someone to point out anything that God gave the church to do that cannot be done through the local congregations divinely ordained.

V. **Scriptural objections to human organizations doing the work of the church.**

1. Human organizations through which to do the Lord's work reflect upon the wisdom of God.

   (1) Since the Lord's church has been designed by the wisdom of God, it is sufficient to accomplish his purposes. When men build human organizations as an aid or substitute for God's organization they evidence their lack of faith in the sufficiency of that which God has provided and their dissatisfaction with God's ways (Isaiah 55:6-9). Men have the same right to write a chapter and add it to the Bible as to build an ante-room on to the church of God.

2. Human organizations supplant the church, usurp the functions God gave it, and ignore the divine pattern.

3. Human organizations defeat the purpose of God that each congregation by functioning according to the divine plan shall be built up to God's glory and honor.

   (1) When human organizations are built to do the work of the church, they rob the church of the strength that would be received by its proper functioning and leave the congregation only the privilege of worship and raising money to subsidize the human institutions that are doing its work.

4. They ignore God's silence and the lack of divine authority and thus violate the will of God by presumptuous sinning.

5. Such organizations are an addition to God's divine arrangement and to his word and do not classify as an aid or expedient in the divine plan.

    (1) Instrumental music is not an aid but an addition because there is no authority for its use. It does not come within the scope of that which God has commanded.

    (2) Human organizations add just as certainly to what God has ordained or authorized as church organization or government. They do not come within the scope of God's commanded arrangement—the congregation.

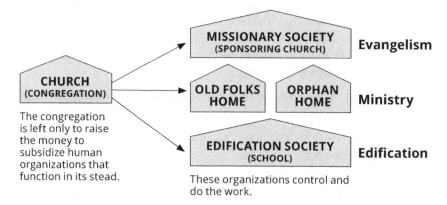

6. Such organizations to do the work of the church or as a medium of cooperation for the churches are without divine authority and are therefore sinful because they violate the principle of walking by faith (2 Corinthians 5:7).

    (1) Faith comes by hearing and hearing by the word of God (Romans 10:17).

    (2) Whatsoever is not of faith is sinful (Romans 14:23).

    (3) Since God's word gives no authority—offers no testimony—to justify human institutions, they cannot be matters of faith, because without hearing there is no faith, and without faith we cannot walk by faith (2 John 9-11).

CONCLUSION

Since God has given by divine wisdom an organization to the church—the congregation—and has made it sufficient to accomplish his purpose, it is the only medium of work and worship through which the Christian can accomplish his purpose and we must be satisfied with his will, his way, and his word.

The Work of the Church—
Evangelism

INTRODUCTION

In Ephesians 4:12, Paul in discussing the purpose of the divine arrangement in the church uses the expression "Unto the **building up** of the body of Christ" (ASV). This is the same word used by Jesus in Matthew 16:18 (*oikodomeo*) when he promised to **build** his church. Paul evidently uses it in the sense of planting, establishing it where it is not known, extending the borders of the kingdom by taking it into new territory or by bringing others into it through the preaching of the gospel. The expression therefore designates the work of evangelizing the world with the gospel of Christ.

I. **It has been God's plan from eternity to save the world by preaching the gospel.**

   1. All mankind in need of salvation (Romans 3:9-10, 23).

   2. The gospel of Christ is God's power to save (Romans 1:16; James 1:21; 2 Timothy 3:15; Acts 20:32; Romans 10:13-15).

   3. Preaching the gospel as a means of saving the lost was planned from eternity (Colossians 1:23-27; Romans 16:25-26; 1 Corinthians 2:7-13; 1 Corinthians 1:21; Titus 1:2-3; 2 Timothy 1:9-11).

II. **The church is God's agency in this work of preaching the gospel.**

   1. The church is taught to observe the commandments of Christ to the apostles (Matthew 28:18-20; Mark 16:15-16—Go teach; preach).

   2. Must contend for the faith once delivered to the saints (Jude 3).

   3. The kingdom or church is the sowing agency (Matthew 13:3-9).

   4. The church is compared to a householder who goes out to hire laborers into the vineyard (Matthew 20:1-16).

   5. The church is the pillar and ground of the truth (1 Timothy 3:14-15).

III. Local congregations were the only organization through which this work of the church was done in New Testament days.

1. The church at Thessalonica was an example to other churches in evangelism (1 Thessalonians 1:3-8).

2. The church in Philippi was outstanding in this work (Philippians 1:3-5; 2:25-30; 4:14-20; 2 Corinthians 11:8-9).

   (1) In all of these instances, they sent to Paul directly—not through a human organization or another church.

IV. No congregation did its work, either evangelism or benevolence, through either a human organization or another congregation.

1. Antioch made up its own contribution and by its own messengers sent directly to the elders of the churches in need in Judea (Acts 11:27-30).

2. Corinth made up its own fund by the contribution of her members, selected her own messenger, and sent it directly to Jerusalem (1 Corinthians 16:1-3).

3. The churches of Macedonia (2 Corinthians 8:2) made up their own funds, chose their own messengers, and sent directly to Jerusalem (2 Corinthians 8:19-23).

4. These same churches of Macedonia sent directly to Paul by the brethren chosen by them (2 Corinthians 11:8-9).

5. Philippi was one of the Macedonian churches, yet acted independently in contributing to Paul through her own messenger, Epaphroditus (Philippians 4:14-18).

6. It is sometimes argued that in 2 Corinthians 11:7-8; Philippians 2:25; 4:14-18, all the churches contribuing to Paul's support sent to Philippi, which as a sponsoring church, sent on to Paul. This contention is based on the statement, "No church communicated with me as concerning giving and receiving but ye only" (Philippians 4:15). The word is *koinoneo*, translated in the King James as "communicated" in Philippians 4:15 and Galatians 6:6. The same form of the word occurs in Romans 12:13; 15:27; 1 Timothy 5:22; Hebrews 2:14; 1 Peter 4:13; 2 John 11, and is translated "distributing" and "partaking." The *koinonia* is more often translated "fellowship" and is so rendered in the American Revised edition in Philippians 4:15.

   The expression "as concerning giving and receiving" is paraphrased by McKnight as follows:

"No church communicated with me in the matter of giving and of my receiving money from them, but ye only."

If Philippi received from other churches and forwarded the funds to Paul—simply keeping books for Paul—in the manner of a "sponsoring church" as some of our modern(-istic) scholars contend today, then the contributing churches had no fellowship with Paul in supplying his needs for such was true only of Philippi. To see this point illustrated, consult the following chart:

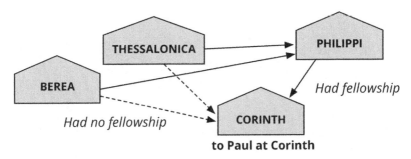

V. **Every congregation did the same kind of work in the same way.**

　1. Paul taught the same "ways" in every church (1 Corinthians 4:16-17).

　2. "So ordain I in all churches" (1 Corinthians 7:17).

　3. "As I have given order to the churches of Galatia, even so do ye" (1 Corinthians 16:1).

VI. **Congregational activity in evangelism did not preclude individual Christian activity in such work.**

　1. Examples of individual activity—private teaching (Acts 5:42; 20:20; 18:24-26).

　2. Evangelists went out of their own accord (Acts 8:5). Men of Cyprus and Cyrene—Acts 11:19-20. Titus—2 Corinthians 8:16-17.

VII. **The church as the only organization designed by the wisdom of God for the work of evangelism does preclude and exclude any other organization or arrangement.**

　1. Since God has given a specific order or arrangement for this purpose, when men form another, they add to God's word and way.

　　(1) God planned the church from eternity to manifest his wisdom (Ephesians 3:8-11).

　　(2) The congregation to hold forth the word of life (Philippians 2:12-15).

(3) The congregation has fellowship with the evangelist in "the furtherance of the gospel" (Philippians 1:5).

(4) Thus fruit abounds to the account of the congregation of saints (Philippians 4:17).

(5) Any substitute order or additonal order for such work arranged by the wisdom and will of man would be a rejection of God's ways.

Lesson 12

The Work of the Church— Edification

INTRODUCTION

The New Testament Scriptures teach that the church of the Lord is a self-edifying body. It is not to be edified through some human educational society or any other human institution but is to edify itself—"unto the edifying of itself in love" (Ephesians 4:16). In Ephesians 4:12, "For the perfecting of the saints" expresses the same idea. The word "edify" means to build up, strengthen, more firmly establish, instruct, or improve. This work of teaching Christians the will of the Lord and establishing them more firmly in the truth that they might be prepared to dwell with him in eternity is certainly a mission of the church.

I. **The church is edified by the strengthening, growth, and development of its members.**

    1. Through that which every joint supplieth (Ephesians 4:16; Colossians 2:18-19).

    2. Do all things unto edifying—the purpose of every Christian (1 Corinthians 14:26; Romans 14:19).

        (1) All things lawful do not edify (1 Corinthians 10:23).

        (2) Impelled by Christian charity one toward another (1 Corinthians 8:1).

    3. Christian duty toward one another (1 Thessalonians 5:11; 2 Corinthians 10:8; Romans 15:1-3).

    4. The congregation is edified and strengthened to the same degree and in the same proportions that its members are developed in Christian character and service and brought into proper relationship with God and with one another (Romans 12:1-11; 1 Corinthians 12:14-27).

II. **The edification of its members is then an important function of the congregation as God designed it (Ephesians 4:11-16).**

    1. The proper objective of a congregation then is not numerical growth alone but the development of spiritual strength (Ephesians 6:10-18).

2. Christians must be strengthened in the faith.

   (1) No longer children tossed to and fro by every wind of doctrine (Ephesians 4:14-15).

   (2) No longer babes fed on milk but of full age and able to take meat (Hebrews 5:12-14).

   (3) Titus charged with this responsibility in Crete (Titus 1:13-2:1).

   (4) Likewise Timothy was so charged in Ephesus (2 Timothy 4:1-5; 2 Timothy 2:14-16; 23-26).

   (5) Grow in grace and knowledge of the faith (2 Peter 3:18).

   (6) In love, knowledge, and all discernment (Philippians 1:9).

   (7) In faith and love (2 Thessalonians 1:3; 3:12).

3. They must grow into godliness and ability to overcome temptation and lead pure lives.

   (1) Establish your hearts unblameable in holiness (2 Thessalonians 3:13).

   (2) Building up yourselves on your most holy faith (Jude 17-23).

   (3) Resist the devil—draw nigh to God (James 4:7-10).

   (4) Ability to serve and sacrifice (Romans 12:1-2).

III. Much of this spiritual growth is to be attained through individual effort.

1. "Study to show thyself approved" (2 Timothy 2:15).

2. "Be strong in the grace that is in Christ Jesus...endure hardship...strive lawfully...consider what I say...remember" (2 Timothy 2:1-8).

3. "Hold fast the form of sound words...heard of me" (2 Timothy 1:13).

4. "Stir up the gift...which is in thee" (2 Timothy 1:6).

5. "Keep that which is committed to thy trust" (1 Timothy 6:20).

6. "Follow after righteousness, godliness, faith, love, patience, meekness. Fight the good fight of faith" (1 Timothy 6:11-12).

7. "These things command and teach...be thou an example...give attendance to reading, exhortation, doctrine...neglect not...meditate...take heed unto thyself" (1 Timothy 4:11-16).

8. "Add to your faith" (2 Peter 1:5-11).

9. "Humble yourselves" (1 Peter 5:6-10).

IV. Christians are to encourage and edify one another.

1. Take thought one for another (Philippians 2:1-4, 19-21).

2. "Exhort one another" (Hebrews 3:12-14; 10:24-25).

3. "Encourage the faint hearted...help the weak" (1 Thessalonians 5:12-14, NASB).

4. "Have fervent charity among yourselves...use hospitality... minister the same one to another" (1 Peter 4:8-10).

5. "Of some have compassion...others save with fear" (Jude 22-23).

6. "If any of you do err...and one convert him" (James 5:19-20).

7. Restore the one "overtaken in a fault...bear ye one another's burdens" (Galatians 6:1-2).

V. Avenues through which the congregation may edify its members.

1. Through worship (Hebrews 10:25; Ephesians 5:19; Colossians 3:16; Hebrews 4:14-16).

    (1) "As lively stones, are built up a spiritual house, an holy priesthood, to offer up spiritual sacrifices" (1 Peter 2:5).

    (2) "Confess your faults one to another, and pray one for another" (James 5:16).

2. Through faithful teaching.

    (1) Originating with Christ and by his authority (Matthew 28:18-20; Ephesians 1:22-23; 1 Corinthians 11:23; 2 John 9-11; Revelation 2:14-17).

    (2) Only apostles had binding and loosing authority (Matthew 16:19; Luke 10:16; 2 Thessalonians 3:6, 14-15; Acts 2:42; Philippians 4:9; 1 John 4:6; 1 Thessalonians 4:8).

    (3) Elders have oversight of the teaching program of the church and are responsible for protecting the church against false doctrine.

        a. They must be apt to teach (1 Timothy 3:2).

        b. "Holding fast faithful word...able by sound doctrine both to exhort and to convince the gainsayers" (Titus 1:9).

        c. Therefore watch (Acts 20:28-31).

        d. They watch for your souls (Hebrews 13:17).

   e. "Whose faith follow...be not carried about with...strange doctrines" (Hebrews 13:7-9).

3. By proper discipline (Titus 3:10; 1 Corinthians 5:1-13; 2 Thessalonians 3:6, 14-15; Romans 16:17-18).

4. By maintaining and encouraging a full program of activity in good works.

   (1) Thus God will bless and enable to do more (2 Corinthians 9:8).

   (2) That fruit may abound to account in heaven (Philippians 4:15-17).

   (3) "Put them in mind...to be ready to every good work...affirm constantly, that they...be careful to maintain good works" (Titus 3:1-8).

   (4) "Charge them...that they be rich in good works" (1 Timothy 6:17-19).

   (5) By each member functioning in his particular capacity for the good of the body (1 Corinthians 12:14-27).

5. Through proper love and consideration of the members one for another (Ephesians 4:29-32; Philippians 4:2; 2:3-4; 1 Corinthians 1:10; 3:3; 8:7-9; 10:23-33; 12:25; Colossians 3:12-15).

CONCLUSION

Whenever any congregation builds and supports some other organization through which to accomplish its work of edification, it becomes guilty of:

1. Avoiding its God-given function.

2. Delegating without divine sanction its own responsibility.

3. Substituting man's way for God's way of discharging its obligation.

The Work of the Church— Benevolence

INTRODUCTION

New Testament teaching on the subject of benevolence needs to be studied in its entirety. It has been a much neglected subject. Many false notions exist in the minds of Christians with reference to the work of the church in this field. It is with the hope that we may come to a renewed understanding and appreciation of the teaching of the Scriptures on this subject that this lesson is offered. The truth concerning this question cannot be determined by sentiment or emotion. Neither can it be learned from what we have done or are doing about such work, because we might be wrong. We can rely only upon the Scriptures to know what God's purposes with the church are in this matter.

I. **The work of benevolence was never used as a means of introducing the gospel or the kingdom of God.**

1. Benevolence is the fruit of Christianity, not the means of propagating it.

    (1) Food and clothing were never offered by the early church as a means of getting people to hear and accept the gospel.

    (2) Paul did not take a contribution of food and clothing with him from the churches when he went to Europe for the first time. There were probably as great a percentage of poor and destitute then as now. The gospel is the power of God unto salvation, and if men will not hear it without being bribed with benevolence, they stand condemned anyway.

2. People who are attracted by benevolence will turn away when the benevolence is discontinued, because their convictions concerning the gospel do not constitute the grounds of their attraction to it.

3. Multitudes followed the Lord for the loaves and fish, physical healing, and the emoluments of political office and reward, but they turned back to walk with him no more the very moment he taught something which they did not like (John 6:66).

II. Much of the teaching in the New Testament on this subject is directed to Christian individuals and not to the congregation.

1. Study these passages: 1 Timothy 6:17-18; Hebrews 13:16; 1 John 3:17-18.

2. Matthew 25:31-46—This passage teaches the absolute necessity of ministering to the needy, whether destitute of food and clothing, sick, or in prison. One cannot go to heaven without ministering to such about him. The picture is one of the judgment. The judgment deals with individuals, according to the works he has done each shall be judged (Revelation 20:11-15; 2 Corinthians 5:10; 1 Peter 1:17).

   We shall not be judged by the benevolence the congregation has done. The individual is not always responsible for what the congregation does or doesn't do. This lesson then concerns individual Christian benevolence.

3. Galatians 6:10—The context of this passage is purely individual. Begin with the first verse and note the terms demanding individual application:

   "Brethren, if a **man** be overtaken in a fault, **ye** which are spiritual, restore **such an one** in the spirit of meekness; **considering thyself, lest thou also be tempted**. Bear **ye one another's** burdens, and so fulfill the law of Christ. **For if a man think himself** to be something, **when he is nothing, he deceiveth himself**. But **let every man prove his own work**, and then shall **he have rejoicing in himself alone, and not in another. For every man shall bear his own burden. Let him that is taught** communicate unto him that teacheth in all good things. Be not deceived, God is not mocked; for **whatsoever a man soweth, that shall he also reap. For he that soweth to his flesh** shall of the flesh reap corruption; but **he that soweth to the Spirit** shall of the Spirit reap everlasting life. And let us not be weary in well doing: for in due season we shall reap, if we faint not. As we have therefore opportunity, let us do good unto all men, especially unto them who are of the household of faith."

   Sometimes it is objected by those who want to apply the teaching of this passage to congregations rather than individuals that "Let him that is taught communicate unto him that teacheth in all good things," if individually applied would justify individual support for teachers. But this is no objection, because the Bible certainly teaches that individuals as well as congregations did support teachers and preachers of the gospel. When the above passage is applied to the church—the congregation—a collective body of Christians, it is wrested from its context or setting and misapplied.

4. James 1:27—Here is another passage that deals with and is addressed to the individual Christian. This is not instruction to the church authorizing congregational action. The entire setting of the passage is individual.

Verse 19:   "Let **every man** be swift to hear, slow to speak, slow to wrath."

Verse 22:   "But **be ye** doers of the word, and not hearers only, deceiving **your own selves**."

Verses 23-25:   "For if **any** be a hearer of the word and not a doer, **he** is like unto **a man** beholding his natural face in a glass; for he beholdeth **himself**, and goeth **his** way, and straightway forgetteth what manner of **man he was**. But **whoso** looketh into the perfect law of liberty, and continueth therein, **he** being not a forgetful hearer, but a doer of the work, **this man** shall be blessed in **his** deed."

Verses 26-27:   "If **any man** among you seem to be religious, and bridleth not **his** tongue, but deceiveth **his own** heart, this **man's** religion is vain. Pure religion and undefiled before God and the Father is this, to visit the fatherless and widows in their affliction, and to keep **himself** unspotted from the world."

It is evident that James is contrasting vain religion with pure and undefiled religion. No one with reason and honesty can ignore the individual application of this passage.

But one has objected that if this passage is not addressed to the church or congregation, then the church cannot practice pure and undefiled religion. In answer to this, we would only suggest that wherever the New Testament Scriptures teach that the churches are to be kept pure, free from the spots and blemishes of the world, and wherever the Scriptures teach the churches to care for the destitute, in such passages the **churches** are taught to practice pure and undefiled religion. But in the above passage, such teaching is addressed to the individual Christian, and to apply it to the churches is to pervert and wrest the passage out of its contextual setting. This, no man has the right to do.

The word "visit" in this passage does not mean just going by to see these destitute widows and fatherless. It embraces the idea of ascertaining their needs and supplying them—ministering unto them.

5. There are many reasons why the individual Christian should do this work himself and not by proxy by simply paying someone to do it for him.

    (1) Such work makes one Christlike. Jesus went about doing good (Acts 10:38). "The Son of man came not to be ministered unto but to minister" (Mark 10:45). "Christ suffered for us, leaving us an example" (1 Peter 2:21).

    (2) Personal contact with the destitute and their needs and the personal strength that comes by ministering unto them is designed for the development of our souls, and in it we find a blessing (Acts 20:35-36; Titus 3:8).

    (3) Our eternal destiny depends upon it (Matthew 25:31-46).

6. The individual Christian is charged with the care of those who are in his own family and therefore have the right to depend upon him for sustenance.

    (1) Those who do not care for their own are worse than infidels (1 Timothy 5:8).

    (2) The church cannot assume the obligation of the individual (1 Timothy 5:16).

        Note: It would be revealing to know how many of the aged in the institutions built and maintained by the churches are the responsibility of individual Christians honored and fellowshipped by the churches in spite of such sin.

    (3) Jesus condemned the Jews for this very sin (Matthew 15:1-9). They were "loosing" or excusing themselves from the obligation to honor—provide for—father and mother, and thus by their traditions making void the commandment of God. Since this is also an obligation under the new covenant, why would it not be just as great a sin today? Yet churches of Christ are excusing those who so sin and have become a party to their sin by accepting the obligation in their stead.

III. God has restricted the benevolent work which the church can do.

1. The church is not to undertake to meet the needs of all humanity.

(1) It could not do so if it tried. The resources of the church would be exhausted before it got started taking care of all the indigent, maimed, mentally incompetent, blind, destitute, disabled, and deserted dependents of society today.

(2) It could not do the work which God has assigned it, if it should undertake such a burden of benevolence. God said for the church not to be charged with the burden of benevolence that belonged to individuals that it might care for those with whose care it has been charged by the divine will (1 Timothy 5:16).

Furthermore, the church is not primarily a relief society, which is what it would become if it were to undertake such a burden of benevolence.

The primary work of the church is spiritual—concerned with the salvation of the souls of men—and to be discharged by the teaching and preaching of the gospel.

The resources of the church are to be devoted to doing the work which God has assigned it and not the work to which men would pervert it.

2. Other agencies in the world are to engage in benevolent work with God's approval and in harmony with his plan, while only the church is to preach the gospel.

(1) The family in the home is charged with caring for its own (Ephesians 6:1-3; 1 Timothy 5:4, 8, 10, 16).

(2) One of the functions for which God ordained civil government is to care for its needy, destitute, and disabled, and for this reason, among others, Christian citizens pay taxes (Luke 20:25).

(3) Only the church is the "pillar and ground of the truth" (1 Timothy 3:15).

3. The only contribution which any congregation made out of its treasury in the New Testament day was to the poor saints.

(1) Romans 15:25-26; 1 Corinthians 16:1-3; 2 Corinthians 8:4; 9:1, 12.

Note: Some have contended that 2 Corinthians 9:13 includes "all men" inasmuch as it reads "and for your liberal distribution unto them, and unto all men." The words "your" and "men" in this passage are interpolations—

supplied by translators. The passage actually says, "unto them, and unto all." The context specifically is talking about the saints and therefore the "all" refers to all the saints and not to all men. There is nothing which indicates anywhere in New Testament teaching that the churches at any time distributed unto all men.

(2) Acts 2:44-45—Here all that believed sold their possessions and goods and parted them to all ("men" is here again interpolated and does not belong in the text), as every man had need. This was not a distribution of general benevolence among all in Jerusalem but was community of property in time of emergency among the believers.

(3) Acts 4:32-35—Here again the context shows that the distribution was among the multitude of them that believed.

(4) Acts 11:27-30—In this instance, the disciples determined to send relief unto the **brethren** which dwelt in Judea.

4. God even limited the saints for whom the church can care in its benevolence.

(1) 1 Timothy 5:1-16—This passage restricts the benevolent work of the church among widows to those who are **widows indeed**. The passage sets forth the following qualifications for a widow indeed who can become the charge of the church.

   a. She must be desolate or destitute.

   b. She must have no one in her family upon which to depend.

   c. She must be faithful in worship.

   d. She must have been godly in life and character.

   e. She must be 60 years of age or above.

   f. She must have been benevolent and faithful in good works herself.

   g. She must have been the wife of one man.

   Note: This passage is not talking about widows who were to be hired or employed by the church as some contend but widows who were subjects of benevolence or relief (1 Timothy 5:16).

(2) Since this passage specifically mentions only widows and since other passages includes the saints as well as the widows, we can be sure that God did not intend to limit the benevolent work of the church to just widows, because of others being included in other instances and passages. The same principles, in so far as they would apply, of course, should be observed by the church in any sustained and continuing program of benevolence at least.

If not, then the passage has no application and hence could not teach us anything. If such limitations do not apply to others, then God discriminated against the widows in the church who are in need.

(3) The reason for such restrictions in the benevolent work of the church is made apparent in verse 16. It is this: the church is not to be burdened with assuming the obligation of benevolence which others should individually discharge or with a general program of benevolence which God did not design for it, but it is to keep its strength and resources free from such obligations that it may do what God intends for it to do. The lesson here is that we are not free to put upon the church what we might consider to be a good work. The church is God's arrangement and should keep herself only to God's purposes and designs and not be prostituted to serve human aims and purposes.

IV. **There is a work of benevolence which the churches of Christ can and should do in harmony with God's will.**

1. The "multitude of them that believed" (Acts 4:32-35) and "all that believed" (Acts 2:44-45) in Jerusalem sold their lands and houses, and pooled or combined their funds in the beginning of Christianity to meet a state of emergency that existed, and "neither was there any among them that lacked" (Acts 4:34).

2. One congregation (Antioch) sent to the relief of the brethren which dwelt in Judea when famine made them destitute.

   (1) This fund was contributed to by the "disciples, every man according to his ability" (Acts 11:29).

   (2) This fund was entrusted to the hands of Barnabas and Saul to be taken where the need existed (Acts 11:30).

   (3) It was sent to the elders among the brethren which dwelt in Judea.

(4) It should be remembered that the brethren which dwelt in Judea constituted the churches of God which in Judea are in Christ Jesus. Hence there was more than one congregation in Judea, and it was the God-ordained plan for every church to have elders (Acts 14:23).

(5) The contributing church sent directly by its own messengers to the churches in need and the benevolence thus contributed was put in the hands of the elders of the local congregation for distribution. This is the divine pattern. If not, there isn't such a thing as a pattern in the Bible for anything.

3. Many congregations—the churches of Galatia, Macedonia, and Achaia—sent to the relief of the Jerusalem church when that congregation had more needy saints than it could care for out of its own resources. Note the following:

(1) The Jerusalem church was obligated to care for its own members.

(2) Due to persecution, their own liberality (Acts 2 and 4), the famine which arose in Judea some fourteen years before (Acts 11:27-30), and perhaps other circumstances, many of the saints in Jerusalem were destitute and there was a greater need than the congregation there could meet.

(3) Other churches were stirred up to supply the want in Jerusalem out of their abundance (2 Corinthians 8:13-14).

(4) The saints in Macedonia besought Paul to allow them to have a part in this work and gave liberally out of their deep poverty of their own accord and because of their deep consecration (2 Corinthians 8:1-5).

(5) Each church made up its fund by the contribution of its own members and not by soliciting money from other churches to enable them to do this work (1 Corinthians 16:1-3).

(6) Each congregation selected and approved its own messenger or messengers to whom this contribution was entrusted for delivery to Jerusalem (1 Corinthians 16:1-4; 2 Corinthians 8:18-23). These messengers were individuals.

(7) The money was sent to Jerusalem where the need existed. The object was to enable the Jerusalem church to care for its own needy saints (2 Corinthians 9:12; Romans 15:26-27). If Paul followed the same pattern which he set in Acts 11:27-30,

this benevolence was delivered to the elders at Jerusalem to be distributed by them.

4. It should be remembered:

(1) In none of these examples did any church set up a benevolent society or institution to care for the needy. It was done under the elders of each church.

(2) No church sent its needy to another church to be cared for. Each church cared for its own and if its obligation to care for its own was greater than it could meet, other churches contributed to this church in need.

(3) No church contributed to another church to enable it to promote and carry on a good work. **They sent only when the church was in need.**

(4) No church handled the money of any other church or became the messenger of any other church.

(5) These examples constitute the pattern for benevolent work among the churches of Christ, just as Acts 20:7 is a pattern of their worship on the Lord's day, and just as Acts 14:23 and Philippians 1:1 constitute a pattern for church organization.

If these examples of how New Testament churches did their benevolent work do not constitute a pattern or model for churches today in doing their benevolent work, then there is no such thing as a pattern for anything in the New Testament. We are left free to worship, organize, and work according to our own will and New Testament examples have no meaning.

The Problems of Congregational Cooperation

INTRODUCTION

There are three solutions to the problem of congregational cooperation that are being offered to the churches of Christ. They need careful study and consideration in the light of Bible teaching without any of the false issues and prejudices that have so commonly been aroused, if a scriptural solution to the problem is to be found. Only the will of God can determine what is right and wrong on the question and God's will can be learned only through a study of his word. There should be complete unanimity of purpose that all the issues in this problem, whatever they are, shall be resolved in the light of divine truth. Every effort should be made in the interest of truth and from such a course we should not allow our minds to be diverted. What saith the Lord? That is the solution to the problem if we are to please God.

I. **The problem cannot be resolved by false standards.**

1. The problem cannot be resolved by the amount of good we may think a particular project is doing.

    (1) We cannot do "evil" that good may come (Romans 3:3-8).

    (2) False doctrines that give false hope may temporarily seem to do some good in the comfort and consolation they offer, but all such seeming good will eventually be lost in God's displeasure at disregard for his word.

    (3) Engaging in unscriptural worship is sometimes justified (?) for the reason that it is "uplifting and inspiring" and does good.

    (4) Anything must be in harmony with the will of God and pleasing to him in order to be good.

2. The fact that we may have practiced a thing for years or even for generations does not justify it in God's sight.

    (1) Jesus condemned the tradition of the Jews which were not in harmony with God's laws without any regard for how long they had held to them (Matthew 15:1-14).

3. "It has been approved by great and wise men in the church."

(1) God has chosen the great things which appear foolish in the judgment of men "that no flesh should glory in his presence" (1 Corinthians 1:25-31; 3:4-7, 18-23). We walk by faith (2 Corinthians 5:7).

4. "It is no more wrong to do a thing, even though it may be done in the wrong way, than it is to do nothing at all."

(1) Evil cannot be compared or classified. The sin of omission is just as evil in the sight of God as the sin of commission and the reverse is also true.

(2) Zeal without knowledge is certainly not pleasing to God (Romans 10:1-3).

(3) God's ways are always best and must be honored (Isaiah 55:6-9).

5. "Men who oppose such a good work have unworthy motives."

(1) God forbids judging the motives and hearts of others (Matthew 7:1-5; 1 Samuel 16:7; Romans 14:10-13).

II. False issues that need to be eliminated.

1. The problem is not whether churches can cooperate but how they can cooperate scripturally.

(1) To charge that those who do not agree with us as to how churches can cooperate scripturally do not believe in any kind of cooperation is to beg the question. Surely there are none who oppose every kind of cooperation. Churches in the New Testament did cooperate—the issue is how?

2. The issue is not how local congregations shall, under their own elders, do their own work as to means or methods which are matters of judgment or expediency to be worked out within the framework of the congregation itself.

(1) The issue is rather that of relationship of congregations to each other in a work for which they are equally responsible and which they undertake concurrently. Is there such a thing as intercongregational functioning or relationship?

3. It is not a question of whether or not the congregation has an obligation to care for its destitute or preach the gospel to the lost and edify the saints, but how congregations can cooperate in fulfilling their obligations to such work.

4. It is not a question of the particular methods or means used in accomplishing such work.

(1) In benevolence, the issue is not the place or house, the necessaries to be furnished, or the supervision to be provided. These are necessary no matter what agency is used to provide them.

(2) The issue in present-day problems is what organization shall provide these necessary arrangements? Shall the church (congregation) do it or shall we build another organization to do it? Will each congregation provide for its own or shall the congregation amalgamate their work, combine their resources, and centralize the control of such work in one eldership? Here is the issue!

III. **Is it scripturally right for congregations of the Lord's church to build and maintain human organizations and to do their work through such organizations as a means of cooperating?**

1. If we have the scriptural right to build human institutions or organizations to do **some** of the work of the churches, then why can't we build, by the same right, such organizations to do **all** of the work of the churches? Further, if we can build such organizations to do the work of **some** of the churches, then why can't we build such organizations to do **all** of the work for **all** of the churches?

   (1) This is the solution to the problem sought more than a hundred years ago and resulted in the United Christian Missionary Society.

2. Such a solution means the churches surrendering control over their work and that means eventually surrendering control over the churches.

   (1) If direct control such as is exercised by the Methodist episcopacy is not developed as a result, then **indirect pressure control** such as is exercised by the Baptist General Convention or the various Baptist Associations will be exercised, and already the facts bear out that our institutions are on the road to such control by recommending and quarantining preachers who will or will not go along with their programs.

3. Scriptural objections to such cooperation:

   (1) The church has no scriptural authority to build anything but the church. Authority is not vested in the church but in Christ, its head, and the church cannot do anything but

that which Christ has authorized it to do. The only thing any congregation has ever been authorized to plant or build anywhere is another congregation of like faith and order through the preaching of the word. To build anything else is to act without scriptural authority (Ephesians 1:22-23; Hebrews 3:4-6).

(2) When the church undertakes to build any organization that God has not ordained and authorized, it reflects upon the wisdom of God. God designed the church. If it is not supreme, perfect, sufficient, complete, and competent to do whatever God would have it to do, then the failure to make such provision would belong to God. Has God made a mistake in planning the church? Are we ready for the conclusions (Ephesians 4:14-16)?

(3) Such a human organization would supplant the church or congregation as an organization, usurp its function by doing its work for it, and nullify God's plan. God planned for the Christian individual to grow and develop, and by building himself up, give strength and vigor to build up the church. When the church seeks to function through some other arrangement, it stifles and destroys its own avenues of development, and its members are denied their proper function and cannot grow and develop. The work of the church has been assigned for our good, and we should do it and not defeat the purpose of God by delegating it to someone or something else (Ephesians 4:12-16; Romans 12:3-9).

(4) The establishment and maintenance of such human organizations by the church is without scriptural authority and is an **addition** to God's will and word, not an **aid**, and is therefore sinful.

Instrumental music is not an aid but the addition of another kind of music to that which God ordained. A human society to do the work of the church, whether evangelistic or benevolent, is an addition to the organization which God has ordained—the congregation—not an aid of that organization. God has ordained the congregation as the one organization through which to do the work of the church.

(5) To build such organizations to do the work of the church without divine authority is to be guilty of the sin of presumption, just like Nadab and Abihu when they brought strange fire to the altar (Leviticus 10:1-2). Other examples

of presumptuous sinning: Uzzah (2 Samuel 6:1-7); Uzziah burning incense (2 Chronicles 26).

(6) To build such organizations to do the work of the church without divine authority violates the principle of walking by faith (2 Corinthians 5:7). Faith comes by hearing and hearing by the word of God (Romans 10:17). We walk by faith and not by sight (2 Corinthians 5:7). Whatsoever is not of faith is sin (Romans 14:23).

IV. **Is it scripturally right for congregations to combine their funds and centralize the control over the use of those funds in one congregation and under one eldership as a means of cooperating in accomplishing their work?**

Note: This type of cooperation is characteristic of the "sponsoring church" arrangement for evangelism. Such churches as Broadway in Lubbock, Union Avenue in Memphis, and Brownfield, Texas have received funds from hundreds of other churches to be spent under their sole direction in mission fields to preach the gospel. It is also characteristic of the Herald of Truth, sponsored and controlled by the Highland church elders in Abilene, Texas, but supported by hundreds of churches throughout the land. There are many others who are also "sponsoring churches," but these mentioned are outstanding examples of churches who promote what they believe to be a good work and gather the funds from any and every church that they can persuade and promote into supporting it.

1. Such an arrangement is a centralized agency for the functioning of the "whole brotherhood" or the "church universal" in exactly the same way as a separate human organization controlled by a board of directors such as is found in a benevolent or missionary society, and is therefore simply a substitute arrangement for such. It simply makes such a society out of an eldership and congregation instead of using some other means.

2. Such an arrangement perverts the function of a congregation by making it a "brotherhood agency" and causing it to function as such instead of a local body as God intended. The work of many churches is concentrated in and controlled by one. If many churches can concentrate a part of their work in one church, then they can concentrate all of their work in one. If not, why not? And if many can concentrate all of their work in one church, then all of the churches can concentrate their work in one church, and all

that is needed is to elect a pope, and we have Catholicism. Where such an arrangement long exists, there will be one.

3. Such an arrangement perverts the office, function, and jurisdiction of an eldership by making a "brotherhood" medium out of them, constituting an agency through which many churches function. God intended that elders should have jurisdiction over the affairs and work of only one arrangement on earth, and that is the local church (1 Peter 5:1-4; Acts 20:28; Philippians 1:1). When many churches operate through one eldership in doing a work, those directing and controlling elders sustain the same obligation and relationship in that work to all the churches supporting it. Whether it is the Herald of Truth broadcast, evangelism in a foreign field, or caring for the orphans of many churches, the obligation of the directing and controlling elders is to take the money from all the contributing churches and any others that want to contribute and use it as wisely, faithfully, and honestly as possible for the purpose for which it is sent. They owe this obligation alike to all churches contributing to the work, not just the one where they are elders. If directing a work sustained by many churches is a part of their function as elders, then in doing so, they become "brotherhood elders," and God is responsible for no such arrangement, neither does his word authorize it.

4. Such an arrangement is a perversion of God's plan and those who preach and teach it are preaching and teaching a perverted gospel. It is insisted that as long as the work is placed under the eldership of one church, all of the constituent elements of a scriptural arrangement are present, because there is no other organization formed. The fact may be that no other organization is formed, but the truth is that the elements—constituent— are changed and perverted into something that God has not arranged (Galatians 1:6-11).

Baptists incorporate into their teaching all of the essentials of the plan of salvation. They believe in faith, repentance, and baptism and require it of those who become a part of their fellowship, but they pervert the order and arrangement God has given by teaching that repentance comes before faith, and salvation before baptism. They have the constituent elements, but they have been perverted (changed) and are not allowed to function in their proper relationship and are therefore wrong.

5. When a congregation and its eldership is made the agency or
    medium through which many churches do their work, it becomes
    an *inter*congregational agency, is no longer in charge of only its
    own *intra*congregational activity, and is acting without divine
    authority.

    When any traffic, work project, or agency operates for several
    states, there must be some authority exercised greater than the
    local state authority. Interstate projects cannot be controlled by
    the authority vested in a single state. So it is true in Christianity,
    when any project operates in or for many congregations, it must
    be controlled by a super-congregation, because it cannot be
    under the control of just a local church. We may make such an
    agency out of a local church and its eldership, but if we do, it will
    be a perversion of the local church and destroy its equality with
    the churches that participate or cooperate with it in the project.

6. Such an arrangement destroys the equality of churches by
    elevating one above another and giving to it power, resources,
    and control which no other possesses. This is not what God
    intended or authorized. Churches are free and equal. There
    is no scriptural classification of churches of Christ. Such an
    arrangement as "sponsoring churches" and "contributing
    churches," whether in name or in fact, is inequality and
    unscriptural.

7. Such an arrangement will eventually destroy the independence
    and autonomy of congregations participating. It is argued that
    this arrangement does not infringe upon the autonomy of the
    local church for the reason that its participation is voluntary.
    That is no argument, because there isn't an arrangement
    or organization in the sectarian world religiously but that is
    voluntary. A. T. DeGroot, professor of church history at Texas
    Christian University in Fort Worth, Texas in his book *Church of
    Christ, No. II* points out that this body of people so denominated
    by him consists of more than a thousand congregations among
    the Disciples of Christ that have either withdrawn from or
    refused to enter and cooperate with the International Convention
    because of their differences concerning the Missionary Society
    Convention method of cooperation.

    The same thing is true of the Baptist Convention, Baptist
    Associations, etc. Only the Roman and Methodist type of
    episcopacy exercises direct control legislatively over the internal
    affairs of churches and over their property. Some of our

evangelistic or missionary arrangements border very closely on that kind of control. Much of the rest of it exercises control over churches and preachers by refusing to endorse, recommend, or even fellowship preachers and churches that will not support their programs. The control is pressure control. There are many instances of outright interference by these "brotherhood agencies"—all of them—in churches employing certain preachers or using them for meetings. Many such can be established and it will grow worse as the use of such "cooperation methods" are employed. Control can even be voluntarily yielded.

8. Such an arrangement submits the churches to propaganda and high-powered promotional schemes by super-salesmen employed and sent out to further such cooperation. And we have had in our generation some super-salesmen among the brethren. Witness the fact that a 24-year old boy could promote the churches into a "cooperative movement"—a national broadcast— that threatened until it began to decline to become the most colossal, gigantic, and stupendous enterprise to use advertising slogan and jargon that the church has ever seen.

    Then he turned to a publishing business conducted for the benefit of the brethren and promoted it into approximately $500,000 indebtedness before his creditors caught up with him and threw him into bankruptcy. That is doing big things in a really big way.

    When each ambitious church and ambitious eldership undertakes to promote their own "brotherhood program" and "educate" the brethren to their duty and enlist their help toward success, we will see a grand display of promotional powers, and there will be such activity among all the congregations that are trying to promote all of the other churches out of all the money possible, that we will have time for nothing else.

    Witness the fact that in the recent financial report of the orphan home in San Benito, Texas, the Broadway church of Lubbock, Texas had a contribution to that home listed in the amount of $60, while at the same time they are begging, persuading, and promoting hundreds of other churches out of money to help them support their own orphan home in Lubbock, as well as their other enterprises. When this situation develops, what some of the brethren are calling "reciprocity" will really be in vogue, and all the promoting churches will be sending to all the contributing churches to get them to send back to them, and it will be a grand merry-go-round indeed!

V. There is a divine pattern.

1. As to organization.

    (1) The local church—congregation—subject only to Christ, independent of every other, equal to every other, governing its own affairs through its God-appointed officers. There was no organization larger, smaller, or other than this local body. It is the only organic form God gave the church.

        a. When Paul spoke of "churches of Christ" (Romans 16:16), he referred to many congregations of like faith and order but free and independent of each other. This was likewise true when he wrote to the churches of Galatia.

    (2) The organization of the local church or congregation was fixed by divine authority.

        a. There were elders in every church (Acts 14:23; Titus 1:5; Philippians 1:1).

2. As to cooperation between these local churches.

    (1) One church contributed to another only when the church receiving the contribution was in need (Acts 11:27-30; 1 Corinthians 16:1-4; 2 Corinthians 8:12-15; 9:12-15). There is no New Testament example or teaching, therefore no authority, for one church contributing to another to enable it to do a good work or a big work. Where is the passage?

    (2) When a contribution was sent from the treasury of one church to another needy church or to support the gospel in the work of evangelism, it was always sent directly to the work and never through another church. Each congregation made up its own funds and sent to the work that was being done. Where is the passage that teaches either by precept or example that one church became the agent of another church in forwarding its funds?

    (3) Each congregation selected its own messengers and entrusted its funds to them (1 Corinthians 16:1-4; 2 Corinthians 8:18-19, 23; Acts 11:27-30).

    (4) Individuals were the messengers and not churches (passages cited above).

    (5) The measure of congregational responsibility was the ability of the congregation (2 Corinthians 8:10-12). No congregation had the obligation or right to assume or accept an obligation beyond its ability to perform.

The Pattern of Evangelism

"From the first day until now" (Philippians 1:5).

"Epaphroditus, your messenger" (Philippians 2:25).

The Pattern of Benevolence

"Contribution for the poor saints which are at Jerusalem" (Romans 15:26).

Sent by the "messengers of the churches" (2 Corinthians 8:23).

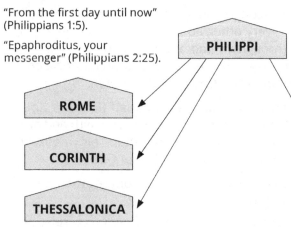

This church had fellowship with Paul by "sending once and again" (Philippians 4:15-17) to his necessity; "supplying that which was lacking" (2 Corinthians 11:8-9).

These messengers were "chosen of the churches" (2 Corinthians 8:19), each church approving its own (1 Corinthians 16:1-4).

The Church Universal and the Church Local

INTRODUCTION

A failure to properly distinguish between the church universal and the church in its local sense is perhaps one of the basic difficulties in the misconceptions and misunderstandings concerning the church and its work as set forth in the teachings of the Scriptures. The Catholic church is the ultimate development in the concept of the church universal as an organic body to function in the performance of its mission in the world.

I. **The term "church" is used in both universal and local sense in the Scriptures.**

 1. Instances of the term "church" used in the universal sense: Matthew 16:18; Ephesians 5:25-27; 1 Timothy 3:15.

 2. Instances of the term "church" used in the local sense: 1 Corinthians 1:2; Romans 16:16; Colossians 4:15-16; Revelation 2:1, 8.

II. **Distinctions to be made between two senses in which the word church is used.**

 1. The church in its universal sense is only a spiritual relationship and not an organization.

 (1) The church is compared to a body, Christ is its head, signifying particularly its relationship to Christ, recognition of his authority, etc. (Colossians 1:18; Ephesians 1:22-23).

 (2) The church is compared to a family, God is the father. "House of God," denoting family (1 Timothy 3:15; Ephesians 2:19).

 (3) The church is compared to a temple in which the Holy Spirit dwells, and therefore denotes relationship to the Spirit (Ephesians 2:21-22; 1 Corinthians 3:16).

 (4) Its members are enrolled in heaven (Hebrews 12:23).

 The church in its local sense is not only a relationship but an organic body or an organization (Philippians 1:1; Acts 14:23). This is the only organic form or existence Christ has given his church on this earth.

    (1) In the local church, the Christian bears a peculiar relationship to the other members of the local body. This is fellowship in its work and worship involving special responsibilities and privileges (Acts 9:26; Romans 16:1-2; 2 John 9-11).

    (2) Fellowship in the local body is subject to its own control (Acts 9:26).

2. The church functions through the local organization and not through any universal medium or organization.

    (1) Ephesians 4:11-12—Here the work of the church—its function—is set forth and the means by which its function is performed. Among those means peculiar to the local church and its organization are pastors (Acts 20:28-32).

    (2) Romans 12:4-8—Here the local church is compared to a body with each member functioning in its own place. The fact that there is a function designated as "he that ruleth" evidences that the function is that of elders and that the figure of "body" is therefore sometimes applied to the congregation or local church. If this passage can be applied to the church universal, as some try to do with the "church as a body" wherever it occurs in Scripture, then those that rule are universal officers rather than congregational officers, and the idea of episcopacy is justified. This obviously is not true. We conclude that the local church is also set forth as a body. As such, it is subject to Christ as its head, and he rules through his authorized representatives who execute his will in the local body.

    (3) Jesus dealt with the seven churches of Asia as separate congregations and announced that he was familiar with works and faults of each as a congregation (Revelation 2 and 3).

The New Testament Scriptures are completely silent as to any universal function of the church and as to any universal organization through which such a function might be performed. If God had intended for the church universal to perform any function upon the earth, is it not self-evident that he would have been wise enough to give it a medium or organization through which to perform that function? The necessary conclusion then is that, since God has given the church only a local organization—the congregation—he intended for its function or work to be executed through the local church as a medium. When we depart from such a medium in trying to serve God in the church, we leave God's plan and become disobedient and irreverent.

3. Fellowship with the saints in the church of the Lord is controlled by the congregation and not by any universal medium or organization.

   (1) The church in Jerusalem did not admit Paul into its fellowship until he was commended by Barnabas (Acts 9:26-28).

   (2) Though Paul had become a Christian through obedience to the gospel, when he came to Jerusalem it was necessary for him to be received into their fellowship as a disciple by the Jerusalem church.

   (3) Paul commended Phoebe to the fellowship of the church at Rome (Romans 16:1-2).

   (4) The church to which John addressed his third epistle wrongfully refused fellowship to certain brethren (3 John 5-10).

   (5) God alone can blot out the names of the saved.

4. Discipline to its members is not administered by any agency of the church universal on earth but rather by the local church.

   (1) Paul instructed the church at Corinth to "deliver unto Satan" the sinful member among them, and it was to be done by them when they were assembled—"when ye are gathered together" (1 Corinthians 5:1-5). There is no way this could be done by the church as a universal body.

   (2) Paul instructed the Thessalonian church to discipline "every brother that walketh disorderly" (2 Thessalonians 3:6, 11-15). This could be carried out only by the local church.

   (3) God is in complete control of discipline administered to the church universal (Revelation 22:19). He also administers discipline to congregations (Revelation 2:5).

      a. The Lord condemns congregations for:

         (a) Departures from true doctrine (Revelation 2:14-15). Commends those faithful to his word (Revelation 3:8-10).

         (b) Condemns those unfaithful in life (Revelation 2:20-23).

         (c) Warns those who have not the right motives and attitude (Revelation 2:5).

         (d) Commends a refusal to accept false authority (Revelation 2:2-3).

(e) Constantly reminds that he knows the works of every church and will judge every church according thereto (Revelation 2:13; 2:2; 2:9; 2:19).

(f) Reminds every church of the necessity to "hear what the Spirit saith to the churches." This will not allow following our own fancy or will but demands the absolute recognition of divine authority (Letters to the seven churches of Asia—Revelation chapters 2 and 3).

Each congregation was directly and independently responsible to the Lord for its own faithfulness to his word and in its work.

Note: It should be remembered that the action of a congregation in withdrawing fellowship from one of its members does not necessarily mean the loss of God's recognition of such member as one of his children. Human beings sometimes err in their efforts even to carry out God's will. Likewise, to be recognized as a member of the church of the Lord in a congregation here on earth does not necessarily mean recognition by God.

5. The individual Christian in fellowship with a congregation shares a relationship and has obligation to that congregation, its elders and members, that he does not have toward any other congregation on earth (1 Corinthians 1:10; Hebrews 10:25; 1 Thessalonians 5:11-15; Titus 1:9-13).

Note: Because an obligation applies universally to all Christians does not even hint that it is to be performed through some universal medium.

II. The local church possesses every attribute and characteristic which is ascribed to the church universal.

1. In Ezekiel's prophetic vision of the temple of God in chapter 40 of his prophecy and in John's vision of the temple in chapter 11 of Revelation, the measuring reed is the word of God, and the temple is the church of God. Most of the scholars agree that both visions must be spiritually applied. In Ezekiel's vision, the temple in its entirety had the same dimensions as each "little chamber" therein. A physical or material building could not possibly have such characteristics.

2. The Christian in the congregation enjoys every provision of the grace of God, every divine relationship, every privilege, promise, and responsibility that is assigned to the member of the church of God or provided for such.

3. Each congregation constitutes the "body of Christ," the "family of God," the "temple of God," and the "church of Christ" as completely and sufficiently as though it were the only such congregation on earth. If, indeed, there were just the one, it would not lack any characteristic or feature of the church universal. The existence of the church of Christ in any community is in no way dependent upon the existence of another such congregation anywhere on the face of the earth. Such a congregation would not continue to be pleasing to the Lord if it did not plant the church of the Lord elsewhere.

CONCLUSION

In discussion of this lesson it will be interesting to ask for suggestions of any attribute belonging to the church universal that does not characterize the local church that is spiritual in nature.

The Christian's Obligations in the Interest of Unity in the Church

INTRODUCTION

In the midst of any situation, crisis or not, there are certain considerations which the individual Christian is under obligation to keep in mind and discharge in the interest of preserving unity. It is some of these obligations toward unity that we propose to study in this lesson that we may better realize our duty and strive to discharge it fully.

I. **Christians universally have a common faith and enjoy a common salvation, but the problem of unity finds its greatest and most direct obligation in the fellowship of the local church.**

   1. To the Corinthian church Paul directed these demands in the name of Christ:

      (1) "Let there be no division among you."

      (2) "Speak the same thing."

      (3) "Be perfected together in the same mind and judgment" (1 Corinthians 1:10).

      (4) Division is carnal (1 Corinthians 3:3).

      (5) "There should be no schism in the body, but the members should have the same care one for another" (1 Corinthians 12:24-25).

   2. To the Ephesians Paul wrote:

      "With all lowliness and meekness, with longsuffering, forbearing one another in love, endeavoring [making a positive effort in the direction of] to keep the unity of the Spirit in the bond of peace" (Ephesians 4:1-3).

   3. To the Philippian brethren this exhortation:

      "That ye be likeminded, having the same love, being of one accord, of one mind. Let nothing be done through strife or vainglory, but in lowliness of mind let each esteem other better than themselves" (Philippians 2:1-3).

II. **This unity demanded of Christians is an individual obligation.**

1. God condemns the man who brings into the church factionalism
    and division.

    (1) It is walking after the flesh and not after the spirit
        (Galatians 5:19-20).

    (2) Jealousy and faction belong to the wisdom that is earthly and
        are followed by every vile deed (James 3:13-18).

    (3) God's wrath and indignation shall be poured out upon them
        that, because of a factious disposition, obey not the truth
        (Romans 2:8).

    (4) Acceptable worship is nullified by division
        (1 Corinthians 11:17-18).

III. Peace and unity in the body of Christ cannot be bought at the expense of truth and righteousness.

1. Jesus came not to bring peace only but a sword also
    (Matthew 10:34-38). Truth cannot be sacrificed for the sake of
    peace with anybody. Even the closest of human ties must be
    severed when upholding the truth of the Lord demands it.

2. The unity of the Spirit is the only unity that pleases God. It is all
    that is worth keeping "in the bonds of peace" (Ephesians 4:1-7).

3. Those who cause division contrary to the doctrine of Christ are to
    be refused (Romans 16:17-18; 2 John 9-11; Titus 3:10-11).

    Note: When love of the brethren and peace with the brethren
           become so important that we are willing to sacrifice the
           will and word of the Lord for the sake of it, we are more
           interested in peace with men than in peace with God and
           love men more than we love God.

IV. Aside from truth and righteousness and the violation of one's own conscience, the individual Christian should be willing to forego every personal consideration for the sake of peace and unity in the church.

1. In matters of personal opinion and conscience, there should always
    be liberality and generosity toward each other (Romans 14:1-13).
    This passage has to do with matters of personal and private practice
    such as eating of meat. It cannot apply to matters of faith,
    worship, or practice in the church and its work without nullifying
    every principle and requirement of truth in every other passage
    in the New Testament.

2. In matters of personal liberty a Christian is not to consider himself
    to the point of causing his brother to stumble (Romans 14:13-22;

1 Corinthians 8:4-13). A Christian cannot, in the exercise of any personal liberty in the realm of things immaterial to truth and righteousness or in matters of expediency, cause a brother to violate his conscience without sinning (1 Corinthians 8:9-13; 10:23-33). The teaching of these passages can be summed up as follows:

(1) Eating the meat offered in sacrifice to idols was a matter of expediency—immaterial. One who did it was neither the better or worse for having done so (1 Corinthians 8:8).

(2) If one could eat the meat with a good conscience, fully persuaded that it was permissible before the Lord, it was not wrong for him to do so (1 Corinthians 8:4-7; Romans 14:14-23). He who ate meat in violation of his conscience sinned (Romans 14:23; 1 Corinthians 8:7-11).

(3) If one ate the meat with a good conscience but through the exercise of such personal liberty caused his brother to violate his conscience and sin, such an one had not acted charitably (Romans 14:15) toward his brother and, in leading the brother to violate his conscience and sin, had destroyed his brother for whom Christ died and had sinned against Christ (1 Corinthians 8:12).

Note: The sum of this teaching is that every Christian should be ready and willing to leave off any matter of personal liberty and anything in the realm of opinion and expediency for the sake of peace and harmony and for the good of the brethren. This is the way Paul teaches we should "follow after the things that make for peace" (Romans 14:19).

3. A Christian should sacrifice his own judgment and pride in all things not essential to the will of Christ for the sake of harmony and peace (Romans 15:1-2; 1 Corinthians 10:28-33; Philippians 2:3-4; 2:19-22; Colossians 3:12-15; Romans 12:3-5, 16-21).

V. How to avoid division.

1. By uncorrupted doctrine and sound speech (Titus 2:1, 7-8).

2. By having elders who hold to the faithful word and who are able to exhort in sound doctrine and convict gainsayers (Titus 1:9).

3. By leaving off our own speculations, judgments, and opinions, shunning foolish questions, and refusing factious men (Titus 3:9-11).

4. By handling the word of God aright, refusing to strive about words to no profit, and shunning profane babblings (2 Timothy 2:14-18).

5. By refusing ignorant and foolish questions yet dealing in meekness and forbearance with all (2 Timothy 2:23-25).

6. By exercising love and hospitality toward each other yet insisting on speaking as the oracles of God (1 Peter 4:7-11).

7. By refusing to teach private opinions and personal judgments (2 Peter 1:16; 2:2).

8. By all speaking the same thing, and the only way this can be done is for all to confine themselves to matters of faith, divinely revealed (1 Corinthians 1:10).

CONCLUSION

When problems arise that divide the church, every Christian must be sure that his own attitude is right toward God, divine truth, and toward the brethren. In the present crisis in the church over the matter of "congregational cooperation," it is generally agreed by those who offer the **outside organization** (an incorporated benevolent society or organization separate and apart from the church) and those who offer the plan of the **sponsoring church** (the combining of the funds of many churches in one congregation and the centralization of the control over those funds in one eldership) are all on record that these **methods of cooperation** are matters of expediency. They freely admit that there is no authority for them but contend that since God has not specified the "how" of doing his work, we are left free to choose that which is most expedient. If these methods of cooperation are simply matters of expediency and human judgment, then they are not essential, they do not belong in the realm of faith, but are matters of opinion and judgment and are in no way material to the doing of the will of God, since matters of human judgment cannot be bound with the word of the Lord upon the souls of men. If their contention be true in this regard, there are two things taught by the Scriptures cited in the above lesson and many others that could be cited that they have forgotten. They are:

1. No Christian has the right to introduce into the church of Christ any practice in the realm of judgment, opinion, or expediency that creates division and dissention. This is carnality, defiles the temple of God, and will bring destruction upon the person guilty.

2. No Christian has the right to force his opinion or personal liberty upon another in violation of his conscience as a condition of Christian fellowship.

THE APPLICATION

If those brethren who are insisting upon supporting benevolent corporations feel that they must do so in order to meet God's approval, let them do it out of their own funds as individuals until they can learn better and not introduce them into the church and force them upon others who cannot conscientiously support them. When the support of a benevolent corporation is put into the budget of a congregation, if there is a single Christian in that congregation that, as a matter of faith and conscience, cannot contribute to such an institution, he is forced to violate his conscience in order to have fellowship with his brethren or separate himself from fellowship with that congregation in order to keep from violating his conscience.

The same thing is true of the sponsoring church plan of cooperation. When a congregation places the work of another congregation in their budget and thus practices combining the funds of many churches in one church and centralized control and oversight of the use of those funds in one eldership, they force any member of that congregation that cannot participate in such a thing conscientiously, because he does not believe it to be harmony with the word of God, to either violate his conscience in order to have fellowship with the brethren and thus sin against God, or to separate himself from fellowship with such a congregation in order to conscientiously practice what he believes to be right.

Thus churches are being divided and brethren are being led to violate their consciences all over the land because certain other brethren think more of what they admit to be their judgment, opinion, a mere matter of expediency, than they do the church for which Christ died or their brethren for whom he died. They thus sin against their brethren and against Christ.

It is never those who conscientiously oppose such human expediencies as a matter of faith when they are brought into the church that cause division but those who introduce such human expediencies. It was so with instrumental music and the missionary societies and the division they caused. They were justified as matters of expediency and yet introduced into the congregations over the sincere, conscientious protests of many faithful brethren. The attitude of those who introduced them toward their opposition was "you can either accept them or get out." Those who could not sincerely accept them got out. Who caused that division? Everyone knows. It was caused by those who thought so much of their inventions and judgments that they were willing to crucify the church and their brethren in order to have their way. Such had better beware, for the judgment of God rests upon them (1 Corinthians 3:16-17).

Made in the USA
Monee, IL
09 October 2023

44275889R00057